SO-DMV-262

Face to Face with Jesus

Paul Borthwick

John Duckworth

David C. Cook Publishing Co.
Elgin, Illinois—Weston, Ontario

CONTENTS

Sessions by John Duckworth
Options by Randy Southern, Nelson E. Copeland, Jr., and Ellen Larson

About the Authors

John Duckworth is a writer and illustrator in Carol Stream, Illinois. He has worked with teenagers in youth groups and Sunday school, written several books including *The School Zone* (SonPower), and created such youth resources as *Hot Topics Youth Electives* and *Snap Sessions* for David C. Cook.

Randy Southern is an editor of youth products in the Church Ministries division of David C. Cook. He has also written several books including *It Came from the Media* and *Cross Training* (SonPower).

Nelson E. Copeland, Jr. is a nationally known speaker and the author of several youth resources including *Great Games for City Kids* (Youth Specialties) and *A New Agenda for Urban Youth* (Winston-Derek). He is president of the Christian Education Coalition for African-American Leadership (CECAAL), an organization dedicated to reinforcing educational and cultural excellence among urban teenagers. He also serves as youth pastor at the First Baptist Church in Morton, Pennsylvania.

Ellen Larson is an educator and writer with degrees in education and theology. She has served as minister of Christian education in several churches, teaching teens and children, as well as their teachers. Her experience also includes teaching in public schools. She is the author of several books for Christian education teachers, and frequently leads training seminars for volunteer teachers. Ellen and her husband live in San Diego and are the parents of two daughters.

basic session plan would work well for many groups, and you may want to stick with it if you have absolutely no time to consider options. But if you want a more perfect fit, check out your choices.

As you read the basic session plan, you'll see small symbols in the margin. Each symbol stands for a different kind of option. When you see a symbol, it means that kind of option is offered for that step. Turn to the page noted by the symbol and you'll see that option explained.

Let's say you have a small group, mostly guys who get bored if they don't keep moving. You'll want to keep an eye out for three kinds of options: Small Group, Mostly Guys, and Extra Action. As you read the basic session, you might spot symbols that tell you there are Small Group options for Step 1 and Step 3—maybe a different way to play a game so that you don't need big teams, and a way to cover several Bible passages when just a few kids are looking them up. Then you see symbols telling you that there are Mostly Guys options for Step 2 and Step 4—perhaps a substitute activity that doesn't require too much self-disclosure, and a case study guys will relate to. Finally you see symbols indicating Extra Action options for Step 2 and Step 3—maybe an active way to get kids' opinions instead of handing out a survey, and a way to act out some verses instead of just looking them up.

After reading the options, you might decide to use four of them. You base your choices on your personal tastes and the traits of your group that you think are most important right now. **Custom Curriculum** offers you more options than you'll need, so you can pick your current favorites and plug others into future meetings if you like.

(3) *Use the checklist.* Once you've picked your options, keep track of them with the simple checklist that appears at the end of each option section (just before the start of the next session plan). This little form gives you a place to write down the materials you'll need too—since they depend on the options you've chosen.

(4) *Get your stuff together.* Gather your materials; photocopy any Repro Resources (reproducible student sheets) you've decided to use. And . . . you're ready!

The Custom Curriculum Challenge

Your kids are fortunate to have you as their leader. You see them not as a bunch of generic teenagers, but as real, live, unique kids. You care whether you really connect with them. That's why you're willing to take a few extra minutes to tailor your meetings to fit.

It's a challenge to work with real, live kids, isn't it? We think you deserve a standing ovation for taking that challenge. And we pray that **Custom Curriculum** helps you shape sessions that shape lives for Jesus Christ and His kingdom.

—The Editors

Talking to Junior Highers about the Real Jesus

by Paul Borthwick

As youth workers, one of our goals (whether we've articulated it or not) is to combat "dead" religion. We want to teach a faith that is practical, relevant, and life changing. In other words, we want group members to leave our ministries with a sense of the realness of the Christian faith. This is why it is so important to dedicate the weeks ahead to the study of the *real* Jesus.

What does Jesus of Nazareth have to do with junior highers of the 90s? How does this historical figure of two thousand years ago affect a kid going through adolescent challenges and adjustments today?

Whether we acknowledge it or not, one of the questions that junior highers bring to our Sunday school sessions and our youth group meetings is "What difference does Jesus make to *me* and *my* world?"

These studies are designed to help group members see that Jesus is someone who identifies with them in their daily struggles and temptations. As you lead these sessions, however, it is important to keep several issues in mind.

Don't Assume Your Kids Know Much about Jesus

Surveys reveal that many of our young people are quite illiterate with respect to the Bible and Christian history. Many do not know if Jesus lived five hundred years ago or two thousand years ago. Some think that Abraham and Moses were members of the twelve disciples. Was it Jesus who built that ark? How did Jesus kill Goliath?

To find out what group members believe, start by asking questions about Jesus. Their answers may reveal a lack of understanding about basic Christian facts. Responses may indicate certain stereotypes about Jesus' character and piety. Some will think of Jesus as an ethereal spirit-being who knew little about human living. Others may indicate that they wonder if Jesus ever really lived. A few may think He was a religious wimp.

Even if group members know the facts, ask some more questions about the qualities of Jesus. Perhaps the topics in this series can provide the basis for these questions. You may find that your group members do not associate Jesus with courage—after all, some of the pictures of Him seem to indicate a pale, weak individual. Jesus and humor? If He was God, He never laughed, right? What about love? If He never married, how could He know love?

Investigating group members' opinions or thoughts about Jesus will show you the challenges you face as you start this series.

Make Sure You Believe That Jesus Is Relevant Today

Junior highers come with built-in "hypocrisy detectors." They can observe their leaders and discern the difference between the people who *know* the facts and the people who *apply* the facts to their lives.

As a result, the issues of this series should cause us to ask, "Do I know the real Jesus in my own life? Do I know the Jesus who feels my pain, loves me in my weaknesses, inspires me to courage? Before I try to assure group members of Jesus' love and forgiveness, am I sure of it in my own life?"

Perhaps we should review the topics ahead of time and pray, "Lord Jesus, help me to know You better through this series." As leaders, we need to be walking in the direction we are instructing our group members to walk.

Present the Real Jesus, Not a "Problem Free" Jesus

The temptation we all face is to promise that following Jesus will come without cost or inconvenience. In our efforts to relate Jesus' life to our lives, we might be tempted to make the Christian life seem easier than it is.

In the weeks that follow, you will be faced with keeping two truths in balance. On one hand, understanding Jesus' love or friendship will cause you to encourage group members to follow Him with an increased sense that "Christian faith will work for you."

On the other hand, you want to remind group members that we follow Jesus because He is the truth—not just because "it works."

To achieve this balance, focus on the life of Jesus. Walk group members through a passage like Philippians 2:5-11, in which we learn that Jesus made tough decisions—even though it meant short-term pain. Help group members understand that life is not easy for anybody—even Jesus. Show them that Jesus followed God not just because it worked in the short-run but because He was committed to the eternal truth. As a result, He sometimes chose the more difficult path, a fact that all of us will face as we follow Jesus.

Be Alert

In an effort to make Jesus real to your group members, you may find yourself prone to overstate certain truths or oversimplify the faith. Consider three possible temptations which you should be aware of as you enter into this study series.

Temptation #1: To present Jesus' humanity at the expense of His divinity. This problem has faced Christianity through the ages. We want so much to know that "Jesus knows our every weakness" that we forget He was the incarnate Son of God. In an effort to be assured that Jesus identifies with us in our hardships, we remember He was "tempted in every way, just as we are"; but we forget the rest—"yet was without sin" (Hebrews 4:15).

To maintain a balance here, incorporate worship into the sessions on the real Jesus. Remind group members that the Jesus they are learning about is also the Jesus they worship, pray to, and sing praises about. This real Jesus of the Scriptures is alive today and longs to empower us with the qualities of love, courage, and compassion that He exemplified through His life.

Temptation #2: To make Jesus a twentieth-century guy, rather than someone who lived 2,000 years ago. In an effort to make Jesus more "real" to junior highers, you may be tempted to put extra words in His mouth. But no matter how you present the *humor* of Jesus, for example, you must understand that He never would have been invited to do an HBO Comedy Special. And the way that Jesus expressed His feelings in the first century might not be the way that we express our feelings today.

A useful exercise here could involve asking group members questions like, "How do you think Jesus would have demonstrated courage in the world today?" or "In what ways might Jesus have demonstrated love in today's society?"

As we present the eternally relevant Jesus, we can present Him as a person who had all of the qualities descibed in the sessions that follow. But we should make it clear that these qualities were expressed in a way that would be understood in His times and in His culture—demonstrating to us that we must, in the same way, seek to express the qualities of Christ in ways understandable to our times and our culture.

Temptation #3: To present Jesus as being removed from the junior-high context. How do we present a Jesus for junior highers when we know so little about the junior-high Jesus? I have always wished that the Bible told us more about Jesus' adolescent years. What was He like at age thirteen? How did He meet the challenges of maturing? Luke 2:52 indicates the complete nature of His growth, but there is little else written about these years.

This biblical silence can lead us to present a Jesus who was a faithful adult, but who had little to say to junior highers. If junior highers are saying, "But what difference does this make to me?" we want to give them answers.

To do so, look at these sessions that follow through the eyes of your group members. Before each session, ask the questions, "What would I like my group members to learn about this quality of Jesus?" and "How will this quality apply directly to their lives?" Asking such questions will enable you to present a Jesus that junior highers can identify with and follow.

Paul Borthwick is minister of missions at Grace Chapel in Lexington, Massachusetts. A former youth pastor and frequent speaker to youth workers, he is the author of several books, including Organizing Your Youth Ministry (Zondervan).

The images on these two pages are designed to help you promote this course within your church and community. Feel free to photocopy anything here and adapt it to fit your publicity needs. The stuff on this page could be used as a flier that you send or hand out to kids—or as a bulletin insert. The stuff on the next page could be used to add visual interest to newsletters, calendars, bulletin boards, or other promotions. Be creative and have fun!

Who Is Jesus?

Ever wonder what Jesus is really like?
Does He have a sense of humor?
How tough is He?
Does He really care about you?
We'll find answers to these and other questions in our new series called *Face to Face with Jesus*. You might be in for a surprise.

Who:

When:

Where:

Questions? Call:

Face to Face with Jesus

Face to Face with Jesus

Be there—or else!

Why are these people smiling?
Come and find out for yourself!

What's so funny?

Join the adventure!

Does He Feel the Way I Do?

YOUR GOALS FOR THIS SESSION:

Choose one or more

☐ To help kids see that Jesus has strong, human feelings, just as they do.

☐ To help kids understand that they can approach Jesus because He is a real person with warmth and emotion, not an unfeeling historical figure.

☐ To help kids identify feelings they and Jesus have had in common, and to encourage them to draw closer to Him as a result.

☐ Other _____

Your Bible Base:

Matthew 23:13-17; 26:36-46
John 13:33—14:4

Attack of the Androids

(Needed: Electric drill or mixer [optional]; prizes)

Start your meeting with an "android contest." Make sure kids understand that androids are futuristic machines that look human but don't have emotions (as in the *Terminator* movies and *Star Trek: The Next Generation*).

Give volunteers a chance to do their best android impressions in front of the group. Explain that you'll be awarding prizes for the most expressionless face and voice, and the most mechanical movements. To get things going, you may want to assign android contestants to describe your last social event or explain how to get the attention of the opposite sex.

For more fun, add sound effects. As each "android" moves, stand at the back of the room and briefly press the button on an electric drill or mixer to simulate the whine of the android's motors.

After applauding all your androids and awarding prizes, discuss:

What's the difference between an android and a real person? (Androids have no feelings; they don't get sick and don't need food; they don't move as smoothly as we do; they don't have souls; they aren't human.)

Would you want an android as your friend? As your mom or dad? As your son or daughter? Why or why not?

As needed, point out how hard it would be to have a relationship with someone who didn't have feelings—someone who didn't understand our emotions or didn't care for us.

STEP

2

The Messiah's Mask

(Needed: Copies of Repro Resource 1; scissors [optional]; tape)

Before the session, make enough copies of "The Mask" (Repro Resource 1) so that half your group members will have one. Cut out the holes for eyes, nose, and mouth—or bring scissors and let kids cut out the holes themselves.

At this point in the meeting, form pairs. Give one person in each pair a mask and a two-foot piece of cellophane tape to loop around the back of his or her head and fasten the mask in place. Explain that the mask is supposed to represent Jesus, even though we don't know exactly what He looked like.

Then say: **For the next five minutes, those of you with masks are going to play the part of Jesus. Everything you say and do should be the kind of thing you think He'd say and do. You and your partner should make conversation about any subjects you like. Just remember to act like Jesus if you have the mask on; if you don't have a mask, treat your partner as if he or she were Jesus.**

Kids will probably be uncomfortable at first, and may have questions about what to do. But try not to give further guidance. Just watch what they do.

After about five minutes, have kids remove the masks and discuss the experience, using questions like these:
How did it feel to play the part of Jesus? Why?
How did it feel to pretend to talk with Jesus? Why?
In what ways did you change the way you usually act? Why?

For those who wore masks: **Did you show much emotion when you played the role of Jesus? If so, what feelings did you express? If not, why didn't you?**

For those who didn't wear masks: **How did "Jesus" seem to feel about you? Do you think the real Jesus feels that way? Why or why not?**

Chances are that those who played the part of Jesus tried not to laugh or show "negative" emotions or be "undignified." Kids who didn't wear masks may have thought their partners were nice enough, but found it hard to relate to them.

Say something like: **You've probably heard that each of us needs a personal relationship with Jesus. But how do you have a relationship with someone who's so different from you? For instance, does Jesus have normal, human feelings like we do? Or is He like an android, perfect but without emotions? If He is, we'll never get very close to Him. So let's find out what He's really like.**

Heart in Emotion

(Needed: Bibles; pencils; copies of Repro Resource 2)

Distribute copies of "What Did He Do?" (Repro Resource 2). Give kids a few minutes to fill them out individually.

When time is up, reveal that "c" is the answer to every question. Then go over the quiz, asking kids to tell what they know about each of the incidents described. Share as much of the following information as you want to, following up with some of the questions provided. Unless you have extra time, avoid asking kids to look up and read the passages.

(1) Mark 11:15-18 tells how Jesus threw out the people who were turning His Father's house into "a den of robbers." The verses don't say "Jesus was angry," but He obviously was. His reaction was controlled, considering what He *could* have done.

Ask: **Does the idea of Jesus angrily knocking over tables and chasing crooks fit the way you usually think of Him? Why or why not?**

You may want to explain that Jesus' action here doesn't mean that we can go around trashing things we don't like. Unlike us, Jesus is over all human authorities because He is God's Son.

(2) John 11:35 ("Jesus wept") shows Jesus crying over the death of His friend Lazarus and the pain of His friends Mary and Martha. He cried enough that bystanders said, "See how he loved him!" (vs. 36).

Ask: **Do you think Jesus really understands when you feel like crying? Why or why not?**

(3) In Luke 10:21, Jesus is full of joy. So are His disciples, who have just returned from doing miracles in His name. They all feel great, and Jesus responds by praising God.

Ask: **Do you think of Jesus as a happy person? Do you think**

OPTIONS

EXTRA ACTION

LARGE GROUP

HEARD IT ALL BEFORE

LITTLE BIBLE BACKGROUND

MOSTLY GIRLS

EXTRA FUN

MEDIA

SHORT MEETING TIME

SIXTH GRADE

He's ever happy about you? Why or why not?

(4) Jesus was angry with the Pharisees, who were more interested in their rules than in stopping a disabled man's suffering (Mark 3:1-5).

Ask: **Do you ever feel Jesus might be angry with you? If so, when?**

(5) Jesus was angry at the religious leaders, but had tender feelings toward their followers. He even compared Himself to a mother hen wanting to gather its babies to protect them (Matthew 23:37-39).

Ask: **Have you ever wanted to be close to someone, but found that that person didn't want to be close to you? How did you feel? Do you think Jesus ever feels that way about you?**

(6) Matthew 4:2 shows that Jesus felt hungry. He was God, but He was human, too. He didn't use His hunger as an excuse to give in to the devil's temptation (vss. 3, 4), but His stomach really must have been growling.

Ask: **If Jesus understands what it's like to feel hungry, what other feelings might He understand, too?** (Probably other appetites—thirst, the need to be touched, sexual feelings, wanting to be loved, etc.)

(7) Jesus was "in anguish" (intense pain, sorrow, or distress) and sweating heavily as He prayed in the garden of Gethsemane the night before His arrest (Luke 22:39-46). His prayers included "loud cries and tears" (Hebrews 5:7). He was willing to do what God wanted, but knew it was going to be incredibly painful.

Ask: **If you were going through a hard time, would you rather be comforted by someone who had suffered, or someone who had never felt real pain? Which kind of person do you think Jesus is?**

(8) Jesus felt deserted when He was dying on the cross (Matthew 27:32-50). His disciples had run away. His heavenly Father seemed to have turned His back. Shortly before Jesus died, things got so bad that He cried out, "My God, my God, why have you forsaken me?" (vs. 46).

Ask: **Do you think this was the first time Jesus had felt lonely? Why or why not?** (He probably had felt lonely many times— growing up and being "different," being tempted in the desert, being misunderstood by friends and family, etc.)

After discussing the quiz, try the following exercise. Have volunteers read aloud each of the following passages—first without emotion, then with emotions that seem to fit the words:

• Matthew 23:13-17 (Jesus' anger at the Pharisees);
• Matthew 26:36-46 (sadness, loneliness, and pain in Gethsemane);
• John 13:33–14:4 (tenderness toward the disciples).

Then ask: **What does this tell you about Jesus' feelings?** (They must have been strong and real, because what Jesus said doesn't make much sense when you say it without emotion.)

Stop the Action!

Have kids pair up as they did in Step 2. Explain that you're going to describe a situation and that all pairs will act it out until you say, "Stop!" Then read the following:

Your brother or sister has been driving you crazy for a week. Your mom has warned both of you that if she catches you fighting again, you'll both be grounded. Sure enough, your brother or sister tries to start another fight by coming into your room and dropping chocolate chips into your aquarium. Act out what happens.

After about 20 seconds, say, **Stop!** Then discuss:

How does the person you're playing feel right now?

Do you think Jesus ever felt that way? Why or why not?

How do you think He feels about you when you feel that way?

You may want to point out that Jesus grew up with brothers who didn't believe in Him (John 7:5). He knew what it was like to be picked on and treated unfairly, and He knew what it was like to be angry. But He never sinned. So, if He was angry at His brothers, He must have found ways to express it without fighting. When we feel angry, He knows how we feel—but He's probably displeased when we give in to the temptation to fight.

Here's another situation. You're supposed to have a really hard science test today. You and your friend have studied, but you just can't seem to memorize all those chemicals and stuff. The teacher walks into the classroom. Suddenly he announces that he's changed his mind—it's going to be an open-book test, and you can even take it home and work on it together! Act out what happens.

After about 10 seconds, say, **Stop!** Then discuss: **How does the person you're playing feel right now?**

Do you think Jesus ever felt that way? Why or why not?

What do you think Jesus wants you to do when you feel that way?

You may want to explain that Jesus knew what it was like to be happily surprised. When a Gentile soldier showed great faith that Jesus could heal his servant from a distance, Jesus was "astonished" (Matthew 8:10) and pleased. Jesus probably wants us to celebrate pleasant surprises and thank God for them.

Here's one more situation. You're baby-sitting your two-year-old cousin, who's really cute. The two of you are playing with blocks together. Your little cousin is trying hard to build a tall tower, but the blocks keep falling down. Act out what happens.

After about 15 seconds, say, **Stop!** Then discuss:

As the baby-sitter, how do you feel right now?

Do you think Jesus ever felt that way? Why or why not?

How might this situation be like your relationship with Jesus?

You might note that the baby-sitter probably feels a mix of emotions—tiredness over trying to teach the same thing again and again, but feelings of love for the child who's trying so hard. Jesus felt love for a rich man who was trying hard to keep all the commandments and who wanted to know how to have eternal life (Mark 10:21), even though the man wasn't willing to give up his money. It's good to know that Jesus feels love for us when we try to learn from Him and do His will, even when we fail.

To wrap up this step, ask: **If Jesus understands the way you feel and has feelings for you, how could it affect the way you talk to Him?** (You might be less formal, more honest, less scared and guilty about approaching Him, more open about the way you feel, etc.)

How could it affect the way you feel about obeying Him? (You might feel better about obeying a person who cares about you even when you fail.)

How could it affect the way you treat other people? (You might be more careful about others' feelings and more open about your own.)

STEP

5

Meltdown!

(Needed: Heart-shaped object frozen in ice; two buckets; cup; hot water)

Before the meeting, find a small, heart-shaped object (an empty picture frame, plastic locket or jewelry box, etc.). Freeze it in a block of ice. (Suspend it from a string in an empty milk carton; fill the carton with water; and freeze it). Or simply cover the object with ice cubes.

To wrap up the session, display your frozen heart shape in a bucket. Have another bucket filled with hot water nearby. Encourage kids to come by one at a time and pour a cupful of hot water on the block of ice.

As they do, say something like: **Maybe you came to this group thinking that Jesus is pretty cold-hearted—not the kind of person you could relate to. As you pour hot water on the ice, you'll be helping to thaw out the heart shape that's frozen inside. I hope the things we've talked about help to thaw out your image of Jesus, too.**

As long as the heart is surrounded by ice, you can't get to it. But the more you melt the ice, the closer you can get to the heart. It's the same way in your relationship with Jesus. The more you see that He's a real person with real feelings, the closer you can get to Him.

When the ice is finally melted, pass the heart shape around the group. Each person who touches the heart should name a feeling that he or she felt recently—and that Jesus has felt, too. When the heart gets back to you, close in prayer.

The Mask

What Did He Do?

How did Jesus react in each of the following situations? Circle the letter that's next to each answer you choose.

1. **When Jesus saw that merchants were buying, selling, and cheating in His Father's temple, He . . .**
(a) shrugged His shoulders and said, "What can I do?"
(b) told them they would be judged in heaven for their actions.
(c) knocked over tables and benches, chased out the merchants, and stopped anyone who tried to carry merchandise through the temple courts.
(d) snapped His fingers and burned the merchants to a crisp with a bolt of lightning.

2. **After Jesus' friend Lazarus died, Jesus . . .**
(a) said, "That's OK. I'll see him in heaven."
(b) went to the funeral and comforted everyone with Scripture.
(c) cried.
(d) threatened to kill Himself.

3. **When His followers returned happily from a successful assignment, Jesus . . .**
(a) said, "Wipe those smiles off your faces!"
(b) said, "Be not joyful, for therein lies the sin of happiness."
(c) was full of joy Himself.
(d) went out drinking with them.

4. **When some religious leaders didn't want Jesus to heal a man's deformed hand on the Sabbath, Jesus . . .**
(a) told the man to stop whining and use his other hand.
(b) blessed the man and told him to "Come back tomorrow."
(c) got angry and healed the hand anyway.
(d) gave the religious leaders deformed feet.

5. **When He looked at Jerusalem, whose people had killed prophets His Father had sent, Jesus . . .**
(a) called down fire and brimstone, burning the city to the ground.
(b) predicted the fall of the Jerusalem government.
(c) longed to care for the people as tenderly as a hen protects its chicks, if only they would let Him.
(d) felt nothing at all.

6. **After going without food for forty days and forty nights in the desert, Jesus . . .**
(a) was ready for forty more.
(b) did forty push-ups and forty jumping jacks.
(c) was hungry.
(d) grabbed a little boy's lunch of loaves and fish and ate it.

7. **When Jesus faced being arrested and executed, He prayed . . .**
(a) "Thank You that I am about to be crucified."
(b) peacefully and then "slumbered deeply."
(c) with loud cries, tears, and sweat.
(d) that the Roman soldiers would all be struck blind.

8. **When Jesus hung on the cross, dying, He . . .**
(a) looked happily toward heaven.
(b) never said a word.
(c) cried out loudly, asking why God had abandoned Him.
(d) spat on the people who were laughing at Him.

Step 1
Assign the "android" contestants situations that require movement or action: hitting a home run to win a World Series game, robbing a bank, doing a stand-up comedy routine, walking through a haunted house, etc. Emphasize that the contestants should remain as emotionless and mechanical as possible. Putting emotionless characters into emotionally charged situations should result in some funny presentations.

Step 3
Designate each corner of the room "a," "b," "c," or "d" for each question on the quiz. Rather than having kids circle their responses on the quiz, instruct them to go to the appropriate corner. Once kids have chosen a corner, ask them how sure they are of their answer. If they're positive that their answer is correct, they should stand on their tiptoes and stretch both hands above their head. If they're somewhat sure, they should bend over and put their hands on their knees. If they're not sure at all, they should squat down.

Step 2
Depending on how small your group is, you might want to have one person wear the Jesus mask and let the other group members attempt conversations with him or her. Make sure that the person you choose to wear the mask feels comfortable in front of an audience. So that no one feels awkward about talking to "Jesus" in front of everyone else, you might want to hold group conversations, in which "Jesus" fields questions from and/or talks to two or three people at once.

Step 4
Rather than having kids pair up, ask for two volunteers to come to the front of the room and act out each situation. When you "stop the action," ask group members in the audience how each person in the roleplay is probably feeling at that moment. Then discuss whether or not Jesus ever experienced similar feelings. Depending on the number of volunteers you have, you can either switch acting pairs for each roleplay or have the same pair perform all three.

Step 1
Rather than having one person at a time perform his or her android impression in front of the whole group, assign situations that require three or four group members to perform together. Among the situations you might suggest: watching a sporting event (cheering, yelling at the refs, taunting opponents, etc.), moving a piano or some other heavy object, being cheerleaders at a football game, etc. Give each group a minute or two to prepare its presentation.

Step 3
After group members have completed Repro Resource 2, have them divide into three or four teams. As you go over the answers to the quiz, ask the accompanying questions and have the members of each team discuss their responses among themselves. Then have a spokesperson from each team summarize his or her team's responses for the rest of the group.

Step 2

Jaded kids may be particularly susceptible to seeing Jesus as an ultra-serious, emotionless kind of guy who can only be communicated with through reverent, "prayer-like" speech. Emphasize to those who are wearing masks that they should act in the way that they've always been taught Jesus acts. Emphasize to those who aren't wearing masks that they should talk to Jesus in the way that they've always been taught they should speak to Jesus. Afterward, ask volunteers to explain what teachings have affected their view of Jesus and how they communicate with Him.

Step 3

Sometimes teachers who are afraid of presenting Jesus in a "negative light" attempt to explain away His expressions of emotion (particularly in Mark 11:15-18) as being unfathomable, divine actions that have very little similarity to the emotions we experience. It's important in this activity that group members understand that— while Jesus never allowed His emotions to lead to sin—the feelings of anger, grief, and joy He experienced were very much like the emotions we experience today. After discussing each question on the quiz, ask group members to put themselves in Jesus' place and describe how they would have reacted in each situation.

Step 2

If members of your group don't have a clear concept of who Jesus is and what He's like, the mask activity probably won't work well. In its place, you might want to have a group discussion of Jesus' personality. Ask group members to call out words that describe Jesus—particularly those that describe His personality. Emphasize that you're looking for personal opinions here; there are no "right" or "wrong" answers. You might want to question kids regarding their responses, but make sure you don't put anyone on the spot. List group members' suggestions on the board as they are named. Then talk about what it might be like to hang around with someone who exhibited these personality traits. Would it be boring, because He's always serious and talking about spiritual things? Would it be intimidating, because He's perfect? Would it be awkward, because you have nothing in common with Him?

Step 3

Help kids find Matthew and John in their Bibles. Be prepared to assist the readers in pronouncing words like "Pharisees," "hypocrites," "Gethsemane," and "Zebedee."

Step 1

Have kids pair up. Instruct group members to share with their partners one thing that makes them happy, one thing that makes them sad, and one thing that makes them angry. When both members of a pair have shared, they should "compare notes" on their responses. Chances are, group members will find common ground in the things that affect them emotionally. Once group members have begun to identify with each other's feelings, you can introduce the idea of Jesus' being able to identify with our feelings.

Step 5

Celebrate the fact that Jesus can identify with our feelings. Have kids form a circle. Ask each group member to say a short prayer (one or two sentences), praising Jesus for His ability to identify with one specific, emotion-provoking situation. The situations may or may not be personal experiences, but they should be experiences common to most junior highers. For instance, someone might say, "I praise You, Jesus, because You understand our anger when a friend talks about us behind our backs." Someone else might say, "I praise You, Jesus, because You can share in our joy when we get an 'A' on a test."

MOSTLY GIRLS

Step 2
Since it may be difficult for some girls to understand Jesus as relating to all human beings, and not just the guys, encourage them to talk about their questions. After the partners have finished their conversations and the masks have been removed, talk about Jesus, the Son of our Creator, who was fully human and fully God. Say: **It is difficult to understand, but do you think Jesus has the same feelings as all human beings? When you were wearing the mask, did you think you couldn't respond as Jesus would because you are a girl?**

Step 3
After discussing the quiz, ask the girls to form groups of two or three. Have the members of each group choose from Repro Resource 2 the event or emotion that surprised them the most (such as crying or expressing anger) and explain why they were surprised that Jesus would express that feeling.
If group members don't seem surprised by any of the events, try something else. Have the groups choose one event that would most surprise kids who don't know much about Jesus. Then have each group develop a storyboard of that scene, showing several frames of stick figures. Ask: **If this scene were made into a movie, who do you think should play the part of each character? Why?**

MOSTLY GUYS

Step 2
If your guys would be uncomfortable wearing masks and pretending to talk to Jesus, skip the activity. Instead, have group members respond to the following questions: **If Jesus walked into this room right now, how would you act? Would you treat Him like "one of the guys" or would you act differently toward Him? Would you try to talk to Him? If so, what would you talk about? What kinds of things would you avoid talking about? How would talking to Jesus be different from talking to your best friend?** If possible, try to focus discussion on whether Jesus has feelings and emotions similar to ours.

Step 4
Rather than having your group members act out the scenarios, read the situations aloud and ask group members to imagine themselves in each scenario. What feelings would they experience? Do they think Jesus ever experienced similar feelings? How do they think Jesus would feel about them in that situation?

EXTRA FUN

Step 1
If you have time for an additional opener, have group members compete in an "emotion expression" contest. One at a time, have volunteers come to the front of the room and express an emotion (anger, joy, sadness, etc.)—without speaking. Volunteers may use facial expressions, gestures, and body language, but they may not make any sounds. The rest of the group should then vote on which person best displayed each emotion.

Step 3
Have everyone stand up for "A Run through the Emotional Spectrum." Explain that you'll be reading a list of emotional situations. When you read a situation, group members will immediately respond to it in an appropriate way. For instance, if you read a sad situation, group members should frown and pretend to cry; if you read a happy situation, they should smile and laugh; if you read an angry situation, they should scowl and snarl.
Here are some situations you could use:
• **Your pet goldfish just died.**
• **Your teacher just falsely accused you of cheating in front of the whole class.**
• **You just made the varsity basketball team.**
• **Your pet hamster climbed into the washing machine and went through the spin cycle ... but he's OK.**
• **Your best friend told you he or she didn't want to go to a movie with you ... because he or she just got tickets for both of you to see your favorite band in concert.**
• **You just won first prize in a store giveaway—a year's supply of laundry detergent.**

Step 3

Before the session, record some clips of movies and TV shows that present emotion-provoking situations. For instance, you might record an emotional deathbed scene, a scene of a sports team celebrating after a victory, a scene in which bullies are picking on a helpless victim, a scene in which someone is being stalked, etc. Play each scene, and then discuss how Jesus might respond if He faced a similar situation. Emphasize that He would probably experience the same emotions that the characters in the scenes experienced, but that He would never allow those emotions to cause Him to respond in a sinful manner.

Step 5

As your group members melt the block of ice, play a recording of Bryan Duncan's song "You're Never Alone." Ask: **Recognizing that Jesus experienced every emotion you experience, how might that affect the way you respond the next time you get angry? Sad? Fearful? Lonely? Happy?**

Step 1

Rather than allowing everyone to participate in the android contest, simply choose three contestants from the group. (Make sure that the people you choose feel comfortable in front of a group.) Give the contestants one minute to consult with other group members about their routines, and thirty seconds to perform. Afterward, explain to the group the differences between an android and a real person. Then follow up by asking: **Would you want an android as a friend or family member? Why or why not?**

Step 3

Rather than distributing copies of the quiz and giving kids time to fill it out, simply read the questions aloud and have group members respond by raising their hands. Be succinct in explaining each of the eight numbered points. After the session, offer to give copies of the quiz, as well as the accompanying Scripture passages, to anyone interested in further study. For each of the discussion questions, try to limit responses to two or three. (Make sure, however, that you seek out responses from different people for each question.)

Step 1

The urban equivalent of an android is a "crack addict." Improvise by having your teens pretend to act with the lifelessness that comes with being on drugs. In essence, they must become as zombies or the "living dead." If the resources provide, play a spooky tape or record to accentuate the emotionless and inane existence of those who choose drugs over sanity. Shortly thereafter, remind the group that drug addicts often begin their "habits" to escape their deepest emotional hurts, and that Jesus Christ is a *friend* who will help them overcome those hurts.

Step 2

To add a cultural edge to this activity, have your group members begin by coloring the masks with any number of colors they want. Be sure there is a diversity of colorings among the masks. Then explain that the masks are to represent Jesus. Of course, you will hear, "Jesus wasn't yellow, black, red" or whatever colors they have, but continue the game anyway. When it is completed, include a question on what it was like talking to a colorful Jesus. The responses will be varied, but make this point: Jesus loves the diversity of cultures found in the city and radiates from them all. He died for everyone—red, brown, yellow, black, and white. So to be in His presence means to see Him in others (who may look different), and feel and express the emotion of love Christ has for us all.

Step 2

As much as possible, try to pair up a junior higher and a high schooler for this activity. High schoolers probably will be more thoughtful and reverent in the role of Jesus than junior highers will, so try to distribute the masks to high schoolers. Also, junior highers probably will act differently (showing more respect) to "Jesus" if the role is played by a high schooler than they would if it were played by another junior higher.

Step 4

Junior highers may be reluctant to demonstrate their true feelings in the roleplay (for fear of being thought of as childish) if they're paired with a high schooler. As much as possible, try to pair junior highers with other junior highers and high schoolers with high schoolers. Also, with the discussion questions that follow each roleplay, don't ask group members to share their responses with the *whole* group. Instead, have the members of each pair share their responses with each other.

Step 3

Sixth graders may have some difficulty identifying specific feelings from the descriptions. Instead of having group members do Repro Resource 2 individually, have them work in groups of three or four, marking the correct answers and talking together about the feelings expressed. Then as each item is discussed, ask them to name the emotion or feeling and tell whether they also have that feeling.

Step 4

Since it is difficult for some sixth graders to identify with the feelings of the "other" person, talk about how Jesus may have felt if He were a part of the situations in Step 4. Focus on the first two situations and eliminate the third situation about baby-sitting. For the first situation, add questions such as these: **Do you think Jesus would tease His brothers? Why or why not? Is teasing always hurtful?** For the second situation, ask: **How do you think Jesus would express happiness and excitement?**

Date Used: Mon 7/15

Approx.
Time

Step 1: Attack of the Androids 5-7 min
o Extra Action   Pick
o Large Group   3 volunteers
o Fellowship & Worship
o Extra Fun
o Short Meeting Time
o Urban
Things needed:

Step 2: The Messiah's Mask   ✗
o Small Group
o Heard It All Before
o Little Bible Background
o Mostly Girls
o Mostly Guys
o Urban
o Combined Junior High/High School
Things needed:

Step 3: Heart in Emotion 12 min
o Extra Action
o Large Group
o Heard It All Before
o Little Bible Background
o Mostly Girls
o Extra Fun
o Media
o Short Meeting Time
o Sixth Grade
Things needed: photocopies
        pencils

Step 4: Stop the Action! 5-7 min
o Small Group
o Mostly Guys
o Combined Junior High/High School
o Sixth Grade
Things needed:

Step 5: Meltdown! 5-7 min
o Fellowship & Worship
o Media   3 heart
Things needed: objects
        3 small containers

Does He Have a Sense of Humor?

YOUR GOALS FOR THIS SESSION:

Choose one or more

☐ To help kids see that while Jesus isn't a comedian, He did show a sense of humor when He was on earth.

☐ To help kids understand that they can feel comfortable with Jesus because He understands the value of laughter and fun as well as seriousness.

☐ To help kids evaluate their use of humor, in order to follow Jesus' example of using humor to glorify God.

☐ Other _____
_____

Your Bible Base:

Luke 6:20-26, 41, 42; 7:31-35; 12:16-21

Laughing Gas

(Needed: Aerosol can of air freshener with homemade "Laughing Gas" label; team prize)

Before the meeting, get an aerosol can of air freshener. Make a new label that says "Laughing Gas" and tape it on the can.

As each person enters your meeting place, spray a little air freshener in his or her direction. Explain that it's "laughing gas," to help people get in the mood for this session.

Start the meeting with a laughing contest. Form two teams and give each an extra spray with your "laughing gas." Explain that you're going to read a list of "hilarious" words and phrases, and that kids are supposed to laugh after each one. The team that laughs loudest and most sincerely at a word or phrase (you'll be the judge) will win that round. Help kids along with more "gas" as needed.

Here's the list. Insert appropriate words or phrases as directed in brackets.

(1) **Asparagus**
(2) [Name of a school represented in your group]
(3) **Ant farm**
(4) [Name of a group member who's a good sport]
(5) **Hyperbolic paraboloid**
(6) **Mucus**
(7) [Your name]

Give a prize to the team winning the most rounds. Then discuss:

Did your laughter prove that you have a good sense of humor? Why or why not? (No, because it was faked.)

How do you think most of your teachers would have done in this contest? Why?

If you had to choose between a teacher who had a good sense of humor and one who didn't, which would you pick? Why?

Answers will vary, but a sense of humor is valued highly by most kids. They prefer teachers as well as friends who can kid around and take a joke—in other words, who can create an atmosphere in which kids can make mistakes and survive with their self-esteem intact.

Express Yourself

Explain: **I'm going to read a list of well-known people. Let's say that each of these people is going to come and speak to our group. When I mention each one, tell me whether you think he or she has a good sense of humor. But don't tell me out loud. If you think the person's got a great sense of humor, show me a grin. If you think he or she has a so-so sense of humor, frown. If you think the person has no sense of humor at all, put your hands over your face.**

Here's the list. Insert appropriate names as directed in brackets.

(1) [A comedian who's popular with your group]

(2) **The principal of your school**

(3) [An older comedian that kids' parents might like]

(4) [A cartoon character]

(5) **The President of the United States**

(6) **Jesus**

After getting responses, ask kids to explain their reactions to the last name you read. Most kids probably don't think of Jesus as having a great sense of humor, though they may be reluctant to say that. They may say He had a lot of serious work to do and didn't have time to joke around.

Hmm. Haven't we got a problem here? Most of us like our teachers to have a sense of humor. But we're not sure Jesus rates too highly in that department. If Jesus has no sense of humor, how can we get along with Him?

Some kids may suggest that we need to go to Jesus only with serious or important things, and that we can get humor from our friends. If so, ask kids how they feel about teachers who have no sense of humor. Is that the kind of relationship they want with Jesus?

Humorous or Humorless?

(Needed: Copies of Repro Resource 3 cut in half; pencils; Bibles)

Before the session, make copies of "Clash over Comedy" (Repro Resource 3). Cut the sheets in half as indicated.

At this point in the meeting, get kids back into their teams from Step 1. Give the "Debate Team A" half-sheets to one team, and the "Debate Team B" half-sheets to the other.

Say: **Does Jesus have a sense of humor? Team A says no; Team B says yes. See whether you can convince the other team that you're right. Elect a captain for your team, study the Bible verses listed on your sheet, and read the arguments there. Then add any other arguments you can think of that might help you make your point.**

Give teams five to ten minutes to prepare their arguments. Answer questions about procedure if you like, but try to let kids come up with their own arguments. Then have teams make their cases—first Team A, then Team B—for up to three minutes each. Finally, give each team a chance to reply to the other for up to two minutes each.

Let kids comment on whether they personally agreed with their teams' positions, and on whether they were convinced by the other team. Then add the following information as needed:

Team A:

Luke 6:20-26—The world *is* a sad place when you see all the suffering in it. But Jesus' point in verse 25 isn't that laughing (or being well fed) is bad; it's that those who suffer now will someday have a reason to laugh when they're rewarded in heaven. Many who have it easy now will find they have nothing in the next life (vss. 24-26).

Luke 12:16-21—This story is about those who get lots of stuff for themselves but don't care what God wants (vs. 21). Being "merry," like eating and drinking (vs. 19), isn't wrong unless you take it for granted, fail to thank God for it, overdo it, or neglect other things God wants you to do.

We should concentrate on the important work God has for us, as Jesus did. And a lot of people do use humor as a time-waster. But that doesn't mean Jesus is against laughing. His Word says there's a time to cry and a time to laugh (Ecclesiastes 3:4), and "a cheerful heart is good medicine" (Proverbs 17:22).

Team B:

Luke 6:41, 42—This may not seem very funny to us. But Jesus didn't come to earth to be a comedian; He came to be our Savior. He used humor to teach some very serious things. It may be hard to believe that God could have a sense of humor, but the Bible says He knows how to laugh (Psalm 2:1-4).

Luke 7:31-35—If Jesus had no sense of humor, why did people invite Him to parties? Why didn't He hang around with the religious leaders (who took themselves very seriously) instead of with average people?

Maybe the best proof that God—and therefore Jesus—has a sense of humor is that He created us in His image (Genesis 1:27), **and** *we* **have a sense of humor.**

Wrap up the debate discussion by asking: **How could knowing that Jesus has a sense of humor affect your relationship with Him?** (You might look forward more to reading His teachings in the Bible; you might feel friendlier toward Him and less afraid to be yourself when you pray; you might feel more forgiven and less condemned; etc.)

4

It All Fits Together

(Needed: Puzzle pieces copied and cut from Repro Resource 4; envelopes)

Before the meeting, copy and cut enough sets of puzzle pieces from "Making It Fit" (Repro Resource 4) so that you have one set of pieces for every two to four kids. Put each set of pieces in a separate envelope.

At this point in the session, form teams of two to four kids; give each team an envelope of puzzle pieces. Announce that the first team to put its puzzle together will be the winner.

After a few minutes, kids will discover that not all of the pieces fit together. Call a halt to the contest and say: **Let's see why not all of these pieces fit together. Take a look at what's written on them. Put all the Bible verses in a pile on the left, and all the rest in a pile on the right.**

Now look at the pile on the right. What do these questions and comments have in common? (They're all about things that are supposed to be funny.)

What kinds of "funny" things are mentioned on these pieces? (A put-down; a joke based on making fun of a person's religion, disabilities, and race; comedy that uses a lot of swearing; a cruel prank; and a dirty cartoon.)

Why don't these kinds of humor fit with the ideas in the Bible verses? (You can't love your neighbor as yourself and put that person down or be cruel to him or her. If you're stereotyping a whole race, religion, or other group, you're judging. You can't love and obey God and seek His kingdom first while you're doing things—like lusting and using His name in vain—that offend Him.)

Can you imagine Jesus using or liking these kinds of humor? If not, why do some of us get involved with them?

As needed, point out that a lot of us try to put "funny stuff" and "spiritual stuff" in separate piles. We forget that everything in our lives is supposed to fit together. Jesus made sure that His life fit together. He didn't try to hide part of it from God. He used humor to help people get closer to His Father; if it didn't fit that goal, He didn't use it. We should do the same, making sure our use of humor fits God's goals for us.

A Funny Thing Happened . . .

(Needed: Pens or pencils)

Pass out pens or pencils. Ask each group member to take two pieces of the puzzle from Step 4.

Ask: **Remember those "funny" things that didn't fit with the Bible verses? If you need God's help to quit using humor to put people down, or to stop listening to certain kinds of jokes, write on the back of your first puzzle piece a word or phrase about that problem. Use it to help you remember to pray about that problem this week.**

Give kids a moment to do this. Then continue:

If Jesus has a sense of humor, why not share your sense of humor with Him? It may be hard to believe that He'd be interested, but He cares about every part of your life. On the back of your second puzzle piece, write a word or phrase that will remind you to talk to Him this week when something funny happens to you. He'd probably like to hear from you.

Encourage kids to take the puzzle pieces with them. Close in prayer, thanking God for creating humor and for being interested in every part of our lives.

Clash over *Comedy*

Debate Team A

Your Position: Jesus was totally
serious—and we should be, too!
Please read the following verses:
Luke 6:20-26
Luke 12:16-21

Just look at these verses! In Luke 6:20-22 Jesus says the world is a really sad place, and that it's best to cry now, not laugh. He says we're doing well when people hate and insult us. What's funny about that? In verse 25, Jesus comes right out and says, "Woe to you who laugh now." Obviously He's against laughing, so what's the point of telling jokes?

In Luke 12:16-21 Jesus tells a pretty scary story about a man who thought life was all about being "merry" (vs. 19). What happened to him? God called him a fool and killed him. That sums up God's attitude toward humor: It's a waste of time, because we should be concentrating on serious things that will last.

People today think humor is so important, but they're only kidding themselves. They want to escape the real world. Christians shouldn't do that.

We might want to pretend that Jesus was funny so that people today will like Him. But the truth is that Jesus was one of the most serious people who ever lived.

Other arguments you could use:

Debate Team B

Your Position: Jesus showed His
sense of humor—and wasn't
against having fun!
Please read the following verses:
Luke 6:41, 42
Luke 7:31-35

People in Jesus' day had a sense of humor. But they didn't always express it in the words we'd use. Take Luke 6:41, 42, for instance. This may not sound like a joke you'd hear on TV, but it's funny when you think about it. It's like a cartoon—a guy walking around with a big board sticking out of his eye, all bothered about a speck of sawdust in somebody else's eye.

If Jesus had been against telling jokes and having fun, He wouldn't have gone to all those dinner parties with "sinners" (Luke 7:34). Luke 7:31-35 is all about how some people had criticized John the Baptist for being too serious—and then criticized Jesus for not being serious enough.

Jesus had serious work to do, and He wasn't a comedian. But He used humor in his teaching, and He spent time with people who also had a sense of humor. Besides that, Jesus is God—and God created humor when He created everything else!

Other arguments you could use:

MAKING IT FIT

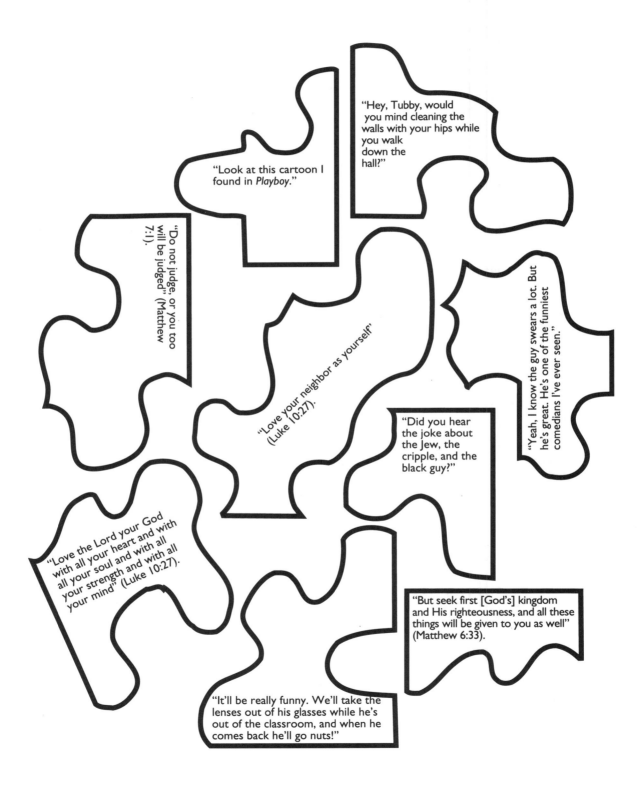

EXTRA ACTION

Step 1

Rather than using just laughter to respond to the list of words, encourage the teams to do *whatever* they can think of to demonstrate hilarity. Some team members may double up from laughter; others may fall out of their seats; and still others may laugh themselves to tears. Award the prize to the team with the most convincing overall display of hilarity.

If you don't think your group members will be able to pull this off, try the opposite. Pair up group members. Have the members of each pair look at each other. Each one should say a word (any word, as long as it's in good taste). The two should continue saying words until one of them smiles or laughs. The first one to smile or laugh loses. Have the winners of each contest pair up and "do battle" again.

Step 4

Add some action to the activity by making it a relay race. Place the envelopes at one end of the room and have the teams line up at the other end. When you say, **Go,** the first member of each team will run across the room, grab one puzzle piece, and bring it back. Then the second person will do the same thing. The teammates continue alternating until all the puzzle pieces have been retrieved. Then they can attempt to put the puzzle together.

SMALL GROUP

Step 1

Choose two or three people who don't mind acting foolishly in front of others and have them compete in a "laugh-off." Read each word on the list, and then give the contestants fifteen seconds to laugh. The rest of the group will then vote on which person laughed the loudest or most hysterically. Award a point to the person who laughs loudest/most hysterically at each word. The person with the most points after all the words have been read is the winner.

Step 3

If your debate teams have only two or three people on them, they may not have enough input to come up with additional arguments to make their points. In that case, you might want to consider sitting in briefly with both teams as they brainstorm, offering suggestions as necessary. But don't just list arguments for the teams to use. Instead, lead them briefly in studying their assigned passages. Ask leading questions to illuminate relevant points. For instance, in Luke 7:31-35, you might ask: **What kind of people usually get invited to parties—boring, "stuffy" people, or people who know how to have a good time?**

LARGE GROUP

Step 2

Have kids divide into groups of five. When you read each name aloud, the members of each group will smile if they think that person has a good sense of humor, or frown if they think the person doesn't have a good sense of humor. If three or more members in a group are smiling, the group must form a smile on the floor by sitting or lying down. If three or more group members are frowning, the group must form a frown on the floor. Have a spokesperson from each group explain his or her group's reasoning.

Step 3

Depending on the size of your group, choose six to eight people (three or four per team) to conduct the debate. Give them five to ten minutes to prepare. While they do, distribute Repro Resource 3 to the rest of the group. Instruct the other group members to read through the sheet, look up the passages, and come up with questions to ask if the debaters fail to address certain points. The object for the rest of the group is to stump the debaters, if possible.

Step 3

Kids who've "heard it all before" may not think of Jesus as having any sense of humor at all. Too often He's portrayed in church solely as the no-nonsense suffering servant who communicated only through dire warnings and complicated parables. If you have a couple of kids in your group who've heard it all before, try to assign them to Team B for the debate. This will give them an opportunity to study Jesus' lifestyle and words in a different light, and may help them recognize that Jesus did indeed have a sense of humor.

Step 4

Have group members look up some other phrases used by Jesus that might demonstrate His sense of humor. Try to find phrases that your group members have probably heard a lot, but never recognized as being "humorous." For instance, you might have them look at Luke 18:24, 25 (try to picture a camel squeezing through the eye of a needle) and Matthew 23:23, 24 (try to picture someone swallowing a camel).

If you don't mind a few groans, you might "announce" that scholars uncovered the following joke in the Dead Sea scrolls.

Jesus: Knock, knock.
Zacchaeus: Who's there?
Jesus: Israel.
Zacchaeus: Israel who?
Jesus: Israel nice to meet you. Now get out of that tree.

Step 2

If some of your group members don't have much Bible background, they may not have an opinion one way or another about Jesus' sense of humor. Take a few minutes to talk with them about their impressions of Jesus. When they think of Him, what kind of person do they picture? An "otherworldly" being in human form who spoke and thought only of serious, heavenly things? A "regular guy" who went to a lot of parties and feasts with people that the religious leaders of the day considered to be "sinners"? A combination of the two?

Bring in some pictures of Jesus from Sunday school curriculum and/or picture Bibles. Have group members determine what emotions Jesus seems to be experiencing in each picture. Ask: **Do you think this is an accurate picture? Why or why not?**

Step 3

For those group members who are unfamiliar with Jesus' use of hyperbole, you may want to explain what Jesus meant by His "speck of sawdust/plank in the eye" comparison. He was emphasizing how foolish and hypocritical it is for us to criticize someone for a fault while remaining blind to our own considerable faults.

Step 2

Have kids pair up and share with their partners how important (on a scale of 1 to 10) humor is to them, and why. When they look for friends, do they look for people who are funny? When they watch TV or movies, do they prefer comedies over other genres? When they're down, would they prefer that someone make them laugh or try to comfort them?

Step 5

Have group members form a circle for closing prayer. Ask each group member to say a short sentence prayer, thanking God for some aspect of humor. For instance, someone might say, "Thank You for giving me friends who make me laugh when I'm down." Someone else might say, "Thank You for giving me a sense of humor, because life would be pretty boring if I had to be serious all the time."

MOSTLY GIRLS

Step 4

After the puzzle pieces have been separated into two piles, have group members form five teams. Distribute one of the "funny" puzzle pieces to each team. Have the members of each team change their comment or joke to reflect what they would say if Jesus were a part of the team, or to reflect what they think Jesus might say. After each team presents its change, talk about how humor fits in with all the other parts of our lives.

Step 5

Talk with your group members about how to respond when humor is used incorrectly or for the wrong reasons. Before they write on their puzzle pieces, have them form teams of three or four and act out one of the "funny" things mentioned on one of the pieces. Ask them to decide how they would respond if someone said to them something similar to what is written.

MOSTLY GUYS

Step 1

Most junior high guys love to tell jokes. So instead of reading the list of words for the teams to laugh at, ask a couple of volunteers to stand up and tell jokes. Emphasize that the jokes must be clean and non-offensive. (If possible, preview the jokes yourself before the volunteers tell them in front of the whole group.) You may want to bring in a good joke book as a resource for your volunteers.

Step 4

For the most part, guys probably are more likely than girls to enjoy—and use—inappropriate humor. Whether it's morning radio "shock jocks," stand-up comedians who do racially and/or sexually inappropriate material, teenage-sex comedies at the movies, or "locker-room" jokes, most teenage guys are exposed to some kind of offensive humor almost every day. Give your group members an opportunity to explain why this type of humor is popular, and to defend it if it's the type of humor they enjoy. If you can create a non-judgmental atmosphere in which kids feel free to share honestly, you'll be better able to have a dialogue with them about appropriate and inappropriate humor.

EXTRA FUN

Step 1

Before the meeting, prepare with one of your funnier group members a presentation on how *not* to be funny. Open the session by having the person come to the front of the room and tell three jokes. On the first joke, the person should mess up the punchline. On the second joke, the person should laugh at himself or herself as he or she tells the joke. On the third joke, the person should stammer, pause, and start over as he or she tells the joke. When the person is finished, lead the group in a standing ovation. Then discuss what it means to have a good sense of humor.

Step 3

Have group members form pairs. Distribute paper and pencils. Give each pair three minutes to write down as many *humorous* ways as it can think of to complete Jesus' statement in Luke 18:25: "It is easier for a _____ to _____ than for a rich man to enter the kingdom of God." For instance, someone might write down "It is easier for (the name of a short girl in your group) to beat Michael Jordan in a game of one-on-one than for . . ." After three minutes, have each pair read its responses. The rest of the group will determine whether a response is humorous or not. Award a prize to the pair with the longest list of humorous responses.

Step 1

Rather than reading the list of words for kids to laugh at, use video clips. Before the session, record seven or eight video scenes. These scenes could include obviously humorous things (i.e., a baby doing something cute) as well as unfunny things (i.e., a traffic light changing colors). No matter what the scene is, however, group members must laugh at it as though it were the funniest thing they've ever seen.

Step 4

Record 30-second clips of several TV situation comedies. Make sure that each clip includes some kind of punchline or one-liner. (But make sure that you don't record any sexually suggestive or risque scenes.) Play the clips for your group members and have them determine whether or not each example of humor is something Jesus would say or do. Use this activity to lead into a discussion of what type of humor we should laugh at and encourage.

Step 1

As group members arrive, divide them into two teams. Then, to start the session, give the teams one minute to laugh (and/or demonstrate hilarity in some other way) as hard as they can. After a minute is up, declare a winner.

Step 3

Rather than dividing into teams for the debate, read aloud each position on Repro Resource 3 and have group members vote on which position they agree with. Ask several of them to explain their reasoning. Be prepared to play "devil's advocate" for each position, to force group members to defend their opinions.

Step 1

For an alternative knock out in laughter, give the teams a chair, a can of "laughing gas" (some kind of aerosol can), and a book. Line the teams up in pairs for a race. Explain that when they see the "gas," they are to laugh. When you say, **Go,** the first pair must run to its chair. One person will center the can of "laughing gas" on the chair and put the book squarely on top of it. The second person will then sit lightly on the book, causing the "gas" to be released from the aerosol can. That pair will then make way for the next pair. The first team finished wins.

Step 4

Another puzzle to consider is one that will help group members learn to laugh at themselves and not be so serious that they cannot experience the humor of being human. This is often important for an urban youth whose image is everything and will fight not to lose his or her "rep"[utation] in the "streets." Give each group member a puzzle piece. Instruct group members to write down one thing they take too seriously. In the weeks that follow, post group members' pieces to symbolize our brokenness and the need to help each other find humor in life.

3 What Kind of Friend Is He?

YOUR GOALS FOR THIS SESSION:

Choose one or more

☐ To help kids see that Jesus was a loyal, caring, down-to-earth friend to His disciples.

☐ To help kids understand that friendship with Jesus starts with obeying Him and grows from there.

☐ To help kids name ways in which they need Jesus to be a friend to them, and to start that friendship by obeying Him.

☐ Other _____
_____

Your Bible Base:

John 15:4-17; 20—21

Magnetic Personalities

(Needed: Index cards; pens or pencils; team prize)

Give each group member an index card and a pen or pencil. He or she should tear the card in half and write a plus sign on one half and a minus sign on the other. Each person should hide half the card in one hand and half in the other so that no one else can see which hand is "plus" and which is "minus."

Form two teams. Each team's members should stand side by side, about arm's length apart. Make sure kids are still hiding their index cards.

Explain: **We're going to play a game called "Magnetic Personalities." You probably know that a magnet has a positive (plus) end and a negative (minus) end. If you put two magnets together, the plus and minus ends will attract each other and stick together. But if you put the plus ends next to each other, they repel—they push each other apart. Same with the minus ends. Opposites attract; likes repel.**

Each of you is now a magnet. You have a plus side and a minus side, based on the cards in your hands. When I say "Attract!" touch your hands to the hands of the people next to you. Then open your hands to see whether you attracted or repelled—based on whether you touched opposites or likes. If you attracted, hold hands. If you repelled, move apart. Ready? Attract!

The team that ends up with the longest unbroken chain of people wins that round. In case of a tie, the team with the most kids holding hands wins that round.

Play a few more rounds, each time giving kids a chance between rounds to switch their plus and minus hands (still hiding the cards) if they wish. Let kids trade places in their lines between rounds if they want to. When the game's over, give a prize to the team that won the most rounds. Then ask:

What do people usually mean when they say that someone has a "magnetic personality"?

Do you think it takes a "magnetic personality" to attract friends? Why or why not?

What kind of person attracts you as a friend?

On the Road Again

(Needed: Backpack and various objects to put in it [see instructions])

Here's a riddle. Based on the clues, who am I talking about?

Clue #1: People in church sometimes sing about what a great *friend* He is.

Clue #2: He was followed around by twelve people He called *friends*.

Clue #3: His enemies called Him a *friend* of sinners.

Group members probably will guess quickly that you're talking about Jesus.

So, tell me about this great friend of yours named Jesus. When was the last time you saw Him?

When you go to McDonald's with Him, what does He usually order?

Does He talk to you on the phone a lot? What did He give you for your last birthday? Do you play catch or Nintendo with Him?

Hey, what kind of friend *is* Jesus, anyway?

Kids probably won't have many answers to the preceding questions. They may even start to wonder whether Jesus is much of a friend after all. That's good, because it's the central issue of this session.

We hear a lot about how Jesus is supposed to be our friend. But what does that mean? What kind of friend can He be to us?

To start with, most of our friends are human beings. We do human-type stuff together. Jesus didn't do that, did He?

Take out a backpack and several items that you've collected before the session. Items should include a fingernail clipper, a bag of chips or some other snack, a harmonica or other small musical instrument, and a towel.

Let's say this is the backpack that Jesus is going to wear on His next hike with the disciples. Which of these things will He need?

Hold up each item and let kids vote on whether to put it in the backpack. Ask them to explain their reasons. As needed, add the following information.

Fingernail clipper—Sure, why not? Jesus had a human body like ours.

OPTIONS

EXTRA FUN

URBAN

His fingernails grew, His hair got longer, His feet got sore.

Bag of chips—They may not have had this snack in Jesus' day, but He ate plenty of other food. He got hungry, just as we do. He ate grilled fish on the beach and bread at the Last Supper. He was always going to dinner at people's houses, and shared a lot of meals with His disciples.

Harmonica—Jesus could have gotten some use from a musical instrument. Singing was one of the things He and His disciples did together (Matthew 26:30).

Towel—Maybe Jesus didn't need one of these for swimming, since He could walk on water (Matthew 14:25). But He used one to clean His disciples' feet after a long, dusty walk (John 13:5).

After putting the items in the backpack, say: **Jesus and His friends shared a lot of the same things we share with our friends— conversation, food, music, work. But is He the kind of friend we would want? Let's find out what it was like to be a friend of Jesus when He was on earth.**

STEP 3

Yearbook Memories

(Needed: Bibles; copies of Repro Resource 5; pens or pencils)

Ask: **Does your school have a yearbook? What kinds of messages do kids write to each other in yearbooks?** (They say how they feel about each other; remind each other of big events they shared; give advice; look forward to seeing each other again; etc.)

What if Jesus had a yearbook with pictures of His friends and the times they spent together? Maybe it would look something like this.

Pass out copies of "Yearbook" (Repro Resource 5) and pens or pencils. Have kids follow the instructions on the sheet. If possible, form four teams—each representing either Peter, Thomas, Mary, or John. Each team should scan the Scripture passage for information about the person it represents, then write messages from that person on the sheets held by members of the other teams.

Before kids scan the chapters, you may want to explain that the disciple described as the one "Jesus loved" (20:2; 21:7, 20) was John, who apparently was especially close to Jesus. You may also want to remind kids that before the events of these chapters, Peter had three times denied knowing Jesus.

OPTIONS

EXTRA ACTION / HEARD IT ALL BEFORE / LITTLE BIBLE BACKGROUND / MOSTLY GIRLS / EXTRA FUN / SHORT MEETING TIME / JR. HIGH HIGH SCHOOL COMBINED / SIXTH GRADE

Allow kids plenty of time to look over the chapters. Then have volunteers share and explain the messages they came up with. As needed, add information like the following.

Peter—Peter's message might recall the amazement he felt over Jesus' resurrection and the incredible haul of fish he got after taking Jesus' advice. Peter probably would apologize for denying Jesus, thank Him for His forgiveness, and promise to "feed [His] sheep" (21:17) (take care of the other disciples and help make new ones).

Thomas—Thomas might also recall the fishing episode. He might express embarrassment over not believing at first that Jesus had been raised from the dead. Probably he would thank Jesus for helping him to believe, and might address Jesus as "My Lord and my God" (20:28) again.

Mary—Mary might mention how sad she felt when it seemed Jesus was gone, and how glad she was to see Him—even how much she'd wanted to hug Him.

John—John probably would have expressed his love for Jesus, the excitement he'd felt when he discovered the empty tomb, and his joy at seeing Jesus again. John probably would have had a lot to write, because he remembered so many events from Jesus' life (21:25).

After discussing the yearbook messages, ask: **Based on what you just read, what words would you use to describe what it was like to be Jesus' friend when He was on earth?** (Some possibilities: exciting, surprising, amazing, strange, hard to believe, busy, etc.)

Jesus' friendships were real. They were full of strong feelings—the kind of feelings that made Mary cry when she couldn't find Jesus (20:11), **and that made Peter jump into the water to get to Jesus** (21:7). **But what about us today? What kind of friendships can we have with Jesus, since He's no longer walking around on earth?**

STEP
4

Fishers of Friends

(Needed: Magnet on a string; mixture of paper clips and pennies)

Have kids stand in their teams from Step 1. Explain that you're going to read a passage about how to be friends with Jesus and with each other. Every time you read the words "remain," "love," "loved," and "friends," kids should clasp hands for one second with those next to

OPTIONS

LARGE GROUP

HEARD IT ALL BEFORE

MOSTLY GUYS

URBAN

them. Every time you say the word "apart," they should move apart.

Before reading, note that Jesus said these things to His disciples, before He was crucified, to prepare them for the time when He would no longer be on earth. So most of the passage applies to us too.

Read John 15:4-17 aloud. Pause when you get to the five aforementioned words so that kids can clasp hands or move apart. As you read, they should clasp hands at least twenty-two times and move apart once.

After reading the passage, discuss the following questions. You may want to have kids look up the passage and refer to it.

Based on these verses, would you say Jesus wants to be close to you or apart from you? (Close, judging from the number of times we clasped hands.)

What does it mean to "remain" in Jesus? (Stay connected to, as a branch needs to stay connected to a vine.)

How do you stay connected with your friends? (Communicate with each other; spend time together; don't let disagreements get in the way; etc.)

How could you stay connected with Jesus? (Pray; read His teachings in the Bible; remember that He's with you wherever you go; ask forgiveness when you do something that would offend Him; etc.)

According to these verses, what's the greatest thing one friend can do for another? (Lay down [give] his or her life [vs. 13].)

Why do you think Jesus mentioned that? (He was about to do that for us.)

What are some things you've given up for your friends?

Say: **So far, friendship with Jesus sounds a lot like friendship with people we know—staying connected, giving things up for their sake. But things change in verse 14.**

Who does Jesus say His friends are? (Those who obey Him.)

Is that what you require of your friends—that they obey you? (Probably not.)

What gives Jesus the right to say that His friends have to obey Him? (He's the Son of God; He knows what's best for us.)

Jesus had started out thinking of His disciples as servants, but ended up thinking of them as friends (vs. 15)**. Why?** (They didn't know much about His business until He taught them.)

Do you have to teach people a lot before they can be your friends? (Usually not.)

What kinds of things might we need to learn before becoming friends of Jesus? (This is a continuing process, but we'd need to learn who He is, what He's done, what He wants of us, how to stay connected with Him, etc.)

Isn't Jesus being a little picky about who can be His friends? Shouldn't He just be friends with everybody?

Let kids respond. If you have time, try the following object lesson to illustrate an answer.

Dump a mixture of paper clips and pennies on a table. Ask a volunteer to come to the front of the room; give him or her a magnet suspended from a string. Ask the person to "go fishing" for paper clips and pennies.

When some paper clips have stuck to the magnet, say: **Hey, have you got something against pennies? Why didn't you pick any up?** (The pennies aren't made of a metal that's attracted to the magnet.)

Thank your volunteer. Then explain to your group members: **The magnet offers the same attraction to everything, but only things that are open to its attraction are picked up. In the same way, Jesus was and is friendly to all kinds of people. But only those who are willing to obey Him will become His friends. Whether you'll be a paper clip or a penny is up to you.**

STEP 5

What, a Friend?

(Needed: Copies of Repro Resource 6; pens or pencils; hymnals and guitar or other accompaniment [optional])

Pass out copies of "Hymn and You" (Repro Resource 6). Encourage kids to fill it out individually. Then let volunteers share what they've written (but don't press).

If your group enjoys singing, supply hymnals and sing all the verses of "What a Friend We Have in Jesus."

Then wrap up the session: **Jesus told His friends, "If you remain in me and my words remain in you, ask whatever you wish, and it will be given you"** (John 15:7). **Are there any things on this handout that you'd like to ask the Lord for? Pick one or two and talk to Him about it now.**

Allow about half a minute for silent prayer. Then close, thanking Jesus for the opportunity to become His friends. If possible, offer to talk later with any group members who want to know more about starting a relationship with Jesus, or who need help with problems they mentioned on their sheets.

O P T I O N S

SMALL GROUP

LITTLE BIBLE BACKGROUND

FELLOWSHIP & WORSHIP

MOSTLY GIRLS

MEDIA

SHORT MEETING TIME

SIXTH GRADE

Yearbook

If Jesus had a yearbook full of memories from His days on earth, what messages might His friends have written in it? After looking at John 20–21, write some notes to Jesus from His friends Peter, Thomas, Mary, and John.

Matthew poses with Future Tax Collectors of Judea Club.

Andrew (3,756th from right) serves loaves and fishes at Annual Feeding of the 5,000 Banquet

PETER

MARY

JOHN

THOMAS

Jesus—
I was up a tree until I met you.
Let's do dinner again.
—Zacchaeus

Jesus—
I'd be dead if it weren't for you. Thanks for everything!
—Lazarus

Step 2

Chances are, your high schoolers and junior highers will have different ideas about what constitutes a great sense of humor. If you think that your junior highers might be reluctant to respond to this activity for fear of being made fun of by the high schoolers, separate the two groups. You may need to think of two different names for #1 and #4—one name appropriate for junior highers and one appropriate for high schoolers.

Step 3

There are two ways to approach the debate with a mixed group. One would be to make sure that each team has an equal number of high schoolers on it. Your high schoolers probably will have more "mature," logical opinions to express (or, at the very least, will be more willing to express their opinions). By splitting up your high schoolers, you're assuring relatively "even" teams. The danger of this approach, however, is that the high schoolers will monopolize the activity. Junior highers may be reluctant to share their opinions in such a setting. The other option would be to have your junior highers debate your high schoolers. If you chose this approach, you probably would want to help the junior highers prepare their presentation.

Step 2

Before reading the list of names, ask your sixth graders to define the term "sense of humor." Have them talk about people who try to make others laugh no matter who or what is hurt in the process, and contrast that with people who are able to see the funny side of things, without hurting others. After the list of names has been read and group members have responded, ask them to identify some people they know who are serious about important things and who also have a sense of humor.

Step 3

Instead of separate debate teams, have the entire group discuss each position and then use a secret ballot vote. Let your sixth graders know that after the discussion they are to vote yes or no about Jesus' sense of humor. Lead the group through the Bible verses on the top half of Repro Resource 3 "Debate Team A" and then do the notes for "Debate Team B." Ask group members to talk about any other events in Jesus' life that would contribute to either position. Have the group members vote on paper; then collect and count the ballots. Present the results and ask for volunteers to explain why they think that position received more votes.

Date Used: _Tuesday 7/16_

Approx. Time

Step 1: Laughing Gas _5 min_
o Extra Action
o Small Group   _lay down_
o Mostly Guys   _w/ head on_
o Extra Fun   _tummy game_
o Media
o Short Meeting Time
o Urban
Things needed: _air freshner_

Step 2: Express Yourself _____
o Large Group
o Little Bible Background
o Fellowship & Worship
o Combined Junior High/High School
o Sixth Grade
Things needed:

Step 3: Humorous or Humorless? _10-12 min_
o Small Group
o Large Group
o Heard It All Before
o Little Bible Background
o Extra Fun
o Short Meeting Time
o Combined Junior High/High School
o Sixth Grade
Things needed:

Step 4: It All Fits Together _10 min_
o Extra Action
o Heard It All Before
o Mostly Girls
o Mostly Guys
o Media
o Urban
Things needed: _photocopies scissors_

Step 5: A Funny Thing Happened ... _5 min_
o Mostly Girls
o Fellowship & Worship
Things needed:

HYMN AND YOU

Here's a song about Jesus' friendship. Maybe you've sung it in church. But have you ever thought about the words?

What a Friend We Have in Jesus

by Joseph Scriven and Charles C. Converse

HYMN

YOU

What a friend we have in Jesus,

Jesus said, "You are my friends if you do what I command" (John 15:14). On a scale of 1 to 10 (with 10 being highest), how good a friend were you to Jesus last week?

_____

All our sins and griefs to bear;

Jesus paid for your sins on the cross. But what's one sin you need Jesus to help you stay away from this week?

_____

What's one "grief" (one thing you feel sad about) that you wish Jesus would help you with this week?

_____

What a privilege to carry Everything to God in prayer.

Are you really so glad about being able to pray that you do it every chance you get? Why or why not?

_____

_____

Oh, what peace we often forfeit;

When you "forfeit" peace, you give it up or lose it (like forfeiting a softball game because you didn't have enough players). One thing that takes away peace is worrying. What's one thing you're worried about this week that you could talk to Jesus about?

_____

Oh, what needless pain we bear;

What problem bothers you the most right now?

_____

Have you prayed about it?

_____

All because we do not carry Everything to God in prayer.

How would you most like Jesus to be a friend to you this week?

_____

_____

EXTRA ACTION

Step 1

Explain that magnetic pull and magnetic repulsion are *constant* energies—they never stop. Your group members must demonstrate this in their actions. If a person "attracts" to another person, the two of them must move back and forth in unison, staying in constant motion. If a person "repels" with another person, he or she must continue bumping into that person and then "repelling" away. Once two or more people are "attracted" together, they will work in unison repelling against others.

Step 3

Rather than having kids *write* their yearbook entries, encourage volunteers to stand up and *speak* them as though they were one of the characters. Don't put anybody on the spot by forcing him or her to stand and share, but encourage most of your group members to participate. Encourage volunteers to "ham it up" by using accents, mannerisms, or any props they can think of.

SMALL GROUP

Step 1

Before the session prepare two halves of an index card for each group member, one half with a plus sign on it and one half with a minus sign. Shuffle the cards well and put them in a pile. When group members arrive, have them draw two cards. (Unlike in the original game, a person may draw two plus cards or two minus cards.) Group members must hold one card in each hand—and they may not show their cards to each other. The object of the game is for group members to align themselves so that at least four people in a row "attract." After each round, collect the cards, shuffle them, and redistribute them. If group members can line up four "attracts" in a row within five rounds, they win a prize.

Step 5

Group members may be reluctant to sing without a lot of others around to "drown them out." If that's the case with your group, bring in a recorded version of "What a Friend We Have in Jesus" and play it while group members work on Repro Resource 6. Encourage kids to meditate on the meaning of the lyrics as they're sung.

LARGE GROUP

Step 1

This activity could serve as an icebreaker for a large group. As group members enter, assign them to a team. Depending on the size of your group, you'll need to have four to six teams. As much as possible, try teaming up kids who don't know each other very well. Give the team members a moment to work together in creating a "strategy" (by arranging themselves according to how they *think* their cards will play). The more you encourage team spirit and unity, the better the "icebreaking" results will be. The winning team in each round gets to stay together. Everyone else must switch teams.

Step 4

If your group members switched teams in the opening activity, form teams for this activity simply by having group members number off one through four (or six, depending on the size of your group). After group members have done the clasping hands-moving apart activity, have them remain in their small groups to discuss the following questions: **What does it mean to "remain" in Jesus? How do you stay connected with your friends? How do you stay connected with Jesus?** Appoint a spokesperson for each team to share his or her group's responses with everyone else.

Step 3

Expand the assignment for Repro Resource 5. Rather than having group members write messages from the four followers based on the events in John 20 and 21, have them write messages that mention at least two specific, personal experiences each character had with Jesus. For instance, Mary might write something like "Thanks again for driving those seven demons out of me. You really know how to change a person's life!" Or Thomas might write something like "Remember when Lazarus died and You and I were the only ones willing to go back to Judea? Those were exciting times." Kids who are familiar with the Bible probably have heard the various accounts at different times, but they may not have a sense of the friendships that were formed with Jesus on the basis of these events.

Step 4

Young people who've been exposed to biblical teaching for most of their lives have probably heard or read this passage several times before. And yet, many of them probably still don't understand what it's saying. To help group members focus on what's actually being taught in the passage, read each verse aloud and then have group members rewrite that verse in their own words. After you've gone through all the verses in the passage, ask volunteers to read what they've written.

Step 3

You may want to provide some additional information about the four followers before group members work on Repro Resource 5. For instance, you might want to explain that Peter, Thomas, and John were Jesus' disciples and that they'd committed the past three years of their lives to following Him. You might briefly discuss Peter's denial of Jesus shortly before Jesus' crucifixion, John's status as "the one Jesus loved," and Mary Magdalene's support of Jesus throughout His ministry (see Luke 8:1-3).

Step 5

Before group members fill out Repro Resource 6, go through the sheet with them, making sure they understand the topics discussed. For instance, do your group members know how Jesus "paid for [their] sins on the cross" and why He had to? Do they know how to "carry everything to God in prayer"? Don't *assume* anything here. If your group members don't have a good grasp of Christian "basics," this activity won't be very effective for them.

Step 1

After each round, give group members one minute for a quick fellowship activity. If two people attracted, they must share with each other one attribute that attracts them to someone else as a friend. If two people repelled, they must share one attribute that might prevent them from starting a friendship with someone else. Each person will have 15 seconds to share. Group members will share with the person on their right first, and then with the person on their left. (The people at each end of the line will share with each other as necessary.)

Step 5

After having sung "What a Friend We Have in Jesus," give kids an opportunity to share their feelings about their friend in a way that's probably familiar to them. Have them pull out Repro Resource 5 again and write their own "yearbook message" to Jesus, praising Him for the things He's done and the effect He's had on their lives. Afterward, give group members an opportunity to share their messages if they want to. (Don't force anyone to share.)

Step 3

Have group members form two additional teams. Explain that these teams will represent two more of Jesus' friends, Martha, and her sister Mary. Instruct these teams to scan John 11 before they write their yearbook messages.

Step 5

Before using Repro Resource 6, ask your group members to talk about their friendship and obedience to Jesus. Ask: **Do you think there are things you cannot or should not discuss with Jesus as a friend because you are a girl? Why or why not? Is obedience to Jesus different for guys than it is for girls? In John 15:4-17, was Jesus just talking to His guy friends or did He mean all people?**

Step 1

Your guys will probably be wary of physical contact with each other. Do not ask them to hold hands for this activity. Instead, you might want to have them put their hands on each other's shoulders. Or you may want to have them just move close to each other, or have them touch feet. Whatever you do, make sure that you don't make your group members feel uncomfortable.

Step 4

As in Step 1, you're going to want to be careful about asking guys to hold hands. Some guys are extremely uncomfortable about physical contact with other guys. Asking them to hold hands with one of their friends or with someone they don't know very well would probably spoil the activity for them and inhibit their learning. So instead of asking them to clasp hands, you should probably have them put their hands on each other's shoulders. Or you may want to have them stand back to back.

Step 2

Bring in several objects—some of them odd, some of them common—and ask volunteers to explain/demonstrate how Jesus might have used them. For instance, He could have used comfortable *athletic shoes* because He and His disciples did a lot of walking. He could have used a *portable grill* because He and His disciples did a lot of outdoor cooking. He could have used a *desk lamp* because He spent a lot of time studying Scripture.

Step 3

Bring in some of your old high school yearbooks for your kids to look at. Spend some time joking about outdated clothing styles, hairstyles, etc. If you think it would be appropriate, let your group members read some of the messages people wrote to you. Use this as a lead-in to the activity on Repro Resource 5.

Step 1

After the game's over, play a recording of Michael W. Smith's classic song, "Friends." Then ask questions like the following: **Do you have a friend who will probably be your friend forever? What do you like about him or her? What does the singer mean when he says, "A friend will not say never, 'cause the welcome will not end"?** Once kids have identified qualities of a "forever friend," you can begin to discuss how Jesus demonstrates those same qualities.

Step 5

Bring in an instrumental recording of "What a Friend We Have in Jesus" as an accompaniment for your group members. Play it a couple of times before your group members sing so that anyone who is unfamiliar with the hymn can learn the tune.

Step 3

Rather than having kids divide into teams to work on Repro Resource 5, work on it together as a group. Briefly summarize the events in John 20–21. Then have group members call out suggestions as to what the four followers might have written in Jesus' "yearbook." You may want to be prepared with a few suggestions of your own to give group members an idea of what you're looking for and to speed up the brainstorming process. For instance, Mary might have written "I can't believe I mistook You for a gardener!" Or Peter might have written "Thanks for the fishing tip. From now on, I'll only fish on the *right* side of the boat."

Step 5

Rather than having kids complete Repro Resource 6 during the session, assign it as "homework." Wrap up the session by reading aloud John 15:7. Then give group members half a minute for silent prayer before you close by praying aloud. As group members leave, hand them a copy of the repro resource and have them fill it out at home—or perhaps before church on Sunday morning (where they could refer to the entire song in a church hymnal).

Step 2

To modify the contents of the backpack in order to be more urbocentrically correct, try some of these items: a Walkman radio, an "X" cap, stone washed jeans, a bus pass, a gold chain, a fashion walking cane, food stamps, and government milk and cheese.

Step 4

If you have an energetic group that loves to dance, bring in a radio with a "stand up and clap" gospel song (or perhaps MC Hammer's renditions of "Do Not Pass Me By" and "Pray"). Instead of having group members clasp hands when they hear the words "remain," "love," "loved," or "friends" in the Scripture passage, you will turn on the music for five seconds and group members will jump, dance, or clap their hands with joy. Include in your discussion afterward the joy and high praise that Jesus imparts into our personal friendships with others and in our spiritual relationship with Him.

Step 1

Since this is a contest that doesn't require skill or knowledge to win, you might want to have your junior highers compete against your high schoolers. Make a big deal about it if your junior highers win. Chances are, they probably usually come up short when they compete with high schoolers. Being able to win even the "Magnetic Personalities" game might give them a needed ego boost.

Step 3

Your junior highers may be unfamiliar with the practice of signing yearbooks. If you suspect that to be the case, ask a couple of your high schoolers to bring in their yearbooks for the junior highers to examine. (You may want to check the yearbooks ahead of time to make sure that the messages are appropriate to be read.)

Step 3

If your sixth graders are not familiar with a yearbook, show them one with handwritten messages in it. Before asking group members to write their own messages, simplify the project by talking about possible ideas of what to write and by identifying specific Bible verses for each group (Thomas—John 20:24-29; Mary—John 20:1, 2, 10-18; John [the "other disciple"]—John 20:2-5, 8, 9; 21:1-14; Peter—John 20:2-7; 21:1-19).

Step 5

Instead of having your sixth graders complete all of Repro Resource 6, ask them to choose three of the "You" questions to respond to. Go over the phrases in the hymn, rewording each one so it is easier to understand. Then talk about the meaning of the words not already described (bear, privilege, needless, carry).

Date Used:

Approx.
Time

**Step 1: Magnetic
Personalities**   _____
o Extra Action
o Small Group
o Large Group
o Fellowship & Worship
o Mostly Guys
o Media
o Combined Junior High/High School
Things needed:

Step 2: On the Road Again_____
o Extra Fun
o Urban
Things needed:

Step 3: Yearbook Memories_____
o Extra Action
o Heard It All Before
o Little Bible Background
o Mostly Girls
o Extra Fun
o Short Meeting Time
o Combined Junior High/High School
o Sixth Grade
Things needed:

Step 4: Fishers of Friends _____
o Large Group
o Heard It All Before
o Mostly Guys
o Urban
Things needed:

Step 5: What, a Friend? _____
o Small Group
o Little Bible Background
o Fellowship & Worship
o Mostly Girls
o Media
o Short Meeting Time
o Sixth Grade
Things needed:

4 Is He Tough Enough?

YOUR GOALS FOR THIS SESSION:

Choose one or more

☐ To help kids see that Jesus took real risks and suffered real pain in standing for the truth and sacrificing His life for us.

☐ To help kids understand that it takes courage to be the people God wants us to be, and that Jesus is our greatest example of courage in action.

☐ To help kids face a specific, threatening situation as Jesus did—by looking beyond the threat to the rewards God has in store.

☐ Other _____

Your Bible Base:

Matthew 26:36—27:50
John 16:31-33
Hebrews 12:2, 3

Indy and Cindy

(Needed: Two copies of Repro Resource 7; felt hat and leather jacket [optional])

Get two volunteers, preferably a guy and a girl, to act out the "Young Indiana James" skit on Repro Resource 7. If possible, loan your Indy a felt hat and leather jacket to wear. The rest of the group can provide sound effects during the skit—water dripping, rats squeaking, snakes hissing, bats flapping, etc.

After the skit, applaud your actors. Then introduce the subject of courage with questions like these:

Who do you think was the bigger coward—Indy or Cindy? Why?

Have you ever been in a really scary situation? What did you do?

What do you think the word "courage" means? (Possible definition: The strength to try something, keep going, or stand up to danger, fear, or difficulty.)

Courage Counters

(Needed: Index cards; pens or pencils; chalkboard and chalk or newsprint and marker)

Before the session, write the following on a chalkboard or piece of newsprint.

1. Making a 20-minute campaign speech to the whole student body
2. Telling your best non-Christian friend how to become a Christian
3. Running into a burning building to rescue a neighbor's child

At this point in the session, distribute index cards and pens or pencils.

Say: **Let's say that each of you has been given ten units of courage to get these three tasks done. The harder a task** would be for you, the more courage units you would need. **Write down how you would divide your ten courage units to complete the tasks. For instance, if making a speech and running into a burning building would be fairly easy for you, you might need only two courage units for each task. That would leave you with six courage units for telling your best friend about Christ.**

Give group members a few minutes to write down on their index cards how they would divide their ten courage units. They must use all ten units, and may not use more than ten.

Then instruct group members to form teams of three, using the following guidelines.

• Each person on a team will be responsible for one of the three tasks. That task should be circled on the person's card.

• The courage units for each team's three circled tasks should add up to ten.

For instance, let's say someone would need five courage units to make a speech. That person might then look for someone who would need three courage units to tell his or her best friend about Christ and someone who would need two courage units to run into a burning building. Together, their courage units add up to ten.

Explain: **The goal for each team is to make sure that all three tasks are covered and that your total courage units needed add up to ten. Go!**

Give kids a few minutes to try to work this out. Chances are, not everyone will be able to form teams of three. When time is up, regather the group and discuss what happened.

How did you do?

Which of the three tasks seemed hardest for most people? Which seemed easiest?

In real life, courage doesn't come in units. Where do you get courage when you need it?

If Jesus were playing this game with us, how many courage units do you think He'd need to do each of the three tasks? Why?

Some kids may suggest that Jesus would use superhuman powers to perform the tasks, so He wouldn't need courage. Try not to judge answers at this point.

Do you think Jesus needed courage to do anything He did while He was on earth? Why or why not?

Answers may vary, which is fine. The point is to get kids thinking about what kind of person Jesus is—and whether the hard things He did on earth might have been hard for Him.

STEP 3

Profile in Courage

(Needed: Bibles; slips cut from a copy of Repro Resource 8; pens or pencils)

I'm going to read a list of statements about Jesus. If you agree with a statement, stay seated. If you disagree, stand up.

• It was easy for Jesus to be brave because He could do anything.

• Jesus wasn't tough—He was gentle and meek.

• Jesus didn't have to be brave because He didn't feel pain like we do.

• It's harder for me to be brave than it was for Jesus, because unlike Him I don't know how things will turn out.

• It takes courage to do things like sharing my faith and standing up for what I believe.

Ask volunteers to explain their reactions to the statements. Then say something like: **A lot of us may figure that Jesus did good things, but that they weren't really *courageous* because He could make things turn out the way He wanted. If that's true, we may wonder whether it's fair for the Lord to ask *us* to do brave things. After all, those things are hard for us! So let's find out the real story about Jesus and courage.**

Pass out the slips you've cut from "Guts and Glory" (Repro Resource 8). Depending on the size of your group, you could give one or more slips to each person, or one slip to each of ten small groups.

Give kids a few minutes to read their passages and to complete the statements. Then bring the group back together and discuss results. Add the following information as needed.

Matthew 26:36-44—Choice to avoid danger or pain: Asking God to cancel the crucifixion, period. Notice that Jesus was so overcome by sadness that He felt like He was already dying (vs. 38). He had the same physical and emotional reactions that most of us would have had. It took courage to keep going, especially when He had no help from His friends. *The choice He made:* Letting God have His way, even if it meant being tortured and killed.

Matthew 26:45-50—Choice to avoid danger or pain: Escaping those who came to arrest Him, maybe hiding out for awhile. *The choice He made:* Going to meet His betrayer and the armed mob.

Matthew 26:50-52—Choice to avoid danger or pain: Trying to fight back, as one disciple (Peter) did. *The choice He made:* To go voluntarily, not using any of His power.

Matthew 26:53-56—Choice to avoid danger or pain: Asking God to rescue Him, and getting help from twelve legions of angels (that's 72,000). He could have chosen to do that at any time, but He didn't. Maybe that was His most courageous act of all. Notice the choice His disciples made—to desert Him. *The choice He made:* To suffer, so that the Bible's predictions about the Messiah would come true.

Matthew 26:57-75—Choice to avoid danger or pain: Giving in to the religious leaders and saying the whole thing had been a misunderstanding. Notice Peter's choice—to pretend he'd never even met Jesus. *The choice He made:* To say the truth, even though it had already gotten Him in trouble—the truth that He is the Messiah, the Son of God. The result was that He was punched, slapped, and spit on.

Matthew 27:1-10—Choice to avoid danger or pain: Escaping the death sentence by getting away from His captors. *The choice He made:* To let Himself be taken away, even though He had just been sentenced to die. Notice the choice Judas made to escape his guilt: suicide.

Matthew 27:11-26—Choice to avoid danger or pain: Explaining to Pilate that the charges against Him were phony, and possibly winning His freedom. *The choice He made:* Not to say anything in His defense. The result: Jesus was flogged, a kind of beating so terrible that victims sometimes died before they could be crucified.

Matthew 27:27-31—Choice to avoid danger or pain: Using His power to keep the soldiers away. *The choice He made:* To let them strip Him, make fun of Him, hit Him, and otherwise abuse Him. Since Jesus had a human body like ours, He felt every bit of it.

Matthew 27:32-44—Choice to avoid danger or pain: Drinking the wine and gall, a painkiller; coming down from the cross to answer the insults of the crowd and the robbers. *The choice He made:* To refuse the drugs; to stay on the cross, suffering incredible pain when He could have come down at any moment.

Matthew 27:45-50—Choice to avoid danger or pain: Coming down from the cross or going directly to heaven to be with His Father, who He felt had abandoned Him. *The choice He made:* To stay on the cross until His sacrifice for us was finished, even though the pain was intense.

If time allows, wrap up this step as follows:

Remember those statements we reacted to by standing up and sitting down? I'm going to read three of them again. How would you reply to them now?

• It was easy for Jesus to be brave because He could do anything. (But He chose not to use His power to escape pain and death—so it was far from easy.)

• Jesus wasn't tough—He was gentle and sort of wimpy. (He was gentle in a way, but it would take a tough person to stand up to the abuse Jesus took.)

• **Jesus didn't have to be brave because He didn't feel pain like we do.** (He felt it all—plus the pain of carrying the whole world's sins.)

STEP 4

Eyes on the Prize

(Needed: Worthless prize)

Ask: **Why do you think Jesus was willing to go through all that pain? Where did His courage come from?**

Listen to responses if there are any. Then say: **We'll look again at that question in a minute. But first let's play a quick game.**

Have kids line up in two teams. Then give the following directions as quickly as you can: **Do twenty pushups. Run fifty laps around the room. Form a human pyramid until you reach the ceiling. Then do one hundred more push-ups, but use only one hand.**

Take a worthless prize (a candy wrapper, chewed piece of gum, etc.) out of your pocket and display it. **And by the way, this is the prize you get if you do everything I just said.**

Chances are that no one will want to play the "game" because the prize isn't worth it.

Would you have tried to play the game if I'd offered you a million dollars? (Probably.)

Jesus was willing to suffer because He knew what the "prize" would be. Look at Hebrews 12:2 and tell me what the prize was. (The "joy set before Him"—saving us from our sins and taking His place of honor next to His Father.)

Look at verse 3. What are we supposed to do? (Remember Jesus' example, and keep going for the prize that awaits us.)

What prize is waiting for us? (Eternal rewards, congratulations from God, etc.)

Doing the brave thing is sometimes rewarded in this life, too. Remember the three tasks we needed "courage units" to do? Refer to the list of tasks on the board from Step 2. **What "prizes" could we get for doing these things?**

(1) Making a 20-minute campaign speech to the whole student body— Possibly winning the election; learning to speak in public; making new friends; feeling more confident around strangers.

(2) Telling your best non-Christian friend how to become a Christian—Learning how to share your faith; having a more honest relationship with your friend; feeling at peace around your friend instead of nervous about witnessing to him or her; maybe helping your friend become a Christian; possibly having the friend with you in heaven.

(3) Running into a burning building to rescue a neighbor's child—Knowing you saved someone's life; learning to trust God; being more confident in scary situations; showing others that being a Christian isn't all talk and no action.

STEP 5

Breaking Down the Door

(Needed: Sheets of cardboard; markers; tape; refreshments)

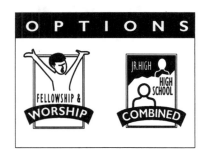

OPTIONS

Before the session, put an assortment of kids' favorite refreshments in a nearby room. Cover the room's doorway by taping sheets of cardboard over it. Make sure kids can't see the refreshments.

At this point in the session, bring kids to the doorway. Give each person a marker or pen.

On these sheets of cardboard, draw a symbol or write a word that stands for a scary or difficult situation you're facing—something you need courage to get through. Just as you don't know what might be on the other side of this door, you don't know what might happen in this situation.

Allow a minute or so for kids to draw or write. Then read aloud John 16:31-33—in which Jesus assures His disciples that He has overcome the world.

Jesus overcame the world because He had the courage to obey God. He was able to do that because He looked forward to the reward that was waiting for Him. What prize might be waiting for you on the other side of the situation you face? Learning something? Accomplishing something? Getting closer to God? Knowing that He's pleased with you? Try keeping your "eyes on the prize" this week.

And remember that we can encourage each other—give each other courage—this week. So let's crash through this doorway together and see what prize is waiting for us on the other side!

After breaking through the cardboard, enjoy your refreshments as a group.

(If you don't have a doorway to use, put the refreshments inside a box and have group members write on the outside of the box. Then, when everyone is finished, open the box and pass out the refreshments.)

Young Indiana James

Characters: *Young Indiana James, adventurer*
Cindy Brandywhine, pampered young heiress

CINDY: Oh, Indy! It's so dark in here! Where are we?

INDY: In the lowest level of the deepest depths of the innermost innards of the Temple of Gloom.

CINDY: Oh, Indy! How will we ever get out?

INDY: Maybe we won't. (*Points toward corner.*) Looks like they didn't.

CINDY: Eeeeek! Skeletons!

INDY: Who's afraid of skeletons? I've got one, and so have you.

CINDY: Oh, Indy! There's something moving around my feet!

INDY: Just some giant rats.

CINDY: Rats? Eeeeeeeeek!

INDY: What's wrong with rats? They make fine pets.

CINDY: Oooh, there's something on my neck!

INDY: Only a crawling heap of tropical fungus beetles.

CINDY: I can't stand bugs! Help!!

INDY: Calm down. They taste great with a little ketchup on them.

CINDY: My hair! Something's in my hair!

INDY: Just vampire bats, rattlesnakes, spiders, eels, pond scum, and broccoli.

CINDY: Noooo! Help!!

INDY: You're such a wimp. OK, I'll get them off you. I'll just light this torch, so I can see better.

CINDY (*Offhandedly*): Did you know you've got a zit on your nose?

INDY (*In a panic*): A zit!? Nooooo-oooo!

CINDY: What's wrong with you? I get zits all the time!

INDY: Why did it have to be a zit? I hate zits! I can't let anyone see me—I've got to get out of here! (*He runs out.*)

CINDY: Get back here, you coward! Some adventurer you are! Take these creepy things off me, or this will be your last crusade!!! (*She runs after him.*)

Guts and Glory

Matthew 26:36-44
The choice Jesus could have made to avoid danger or pain:
The choice He made:

Matthew 26:45-50
The choice Jesus could have made to avoid danger or pain:
The choice He made:

Matthew 26:50-52
The choice Jesus could have made to avoid danger or pain:
The choice He made:

Matthew 26:53-56
The choice Jesus could have made to avoid danger or pain:
The choice He made:

Matthew 26:57-75
The choice Jesus could have made to avoid danger or pain:
The choice He made:

Matthew 27:1-10
The choice Jesus could have made to avoid danger or pain:
The choice He made:

Matthew 27:11-26
The choice Jesus could have made to avoid danger or pain:
The choice He made:

Matthew 27:27-31
The choice Jesus could have made to avoid danger or pain:
The choice He made:

Matthew 27:32-44
The choice Jesus could have made to avoid danger or pain:
The choice He made:

Matthew 27:45-50
The choice Jesus could have made to avoid danger or pain:
The choice He made:

Step 1

Depending on the size of your group, assign three or more people the roles of rat, snake, and bat. Be sure to choose people who aren't afraid to "ham it up" in front of others. Encourage these actors to add as much humor and unpredictability to the skit as possible. For instance, the "rats" might nibble at Indy's and Cindy's legs; the "snakes" might lash out at Indy and Cindy unexpectedly; the "bats" might swoop down on Indy and Cindy throughout the skit.

Step 4

Rather than naming all of the nearly impossible tasks right away, have the teams complete some easier tasks first. For instance, you could instruct them to carry a team member to the far wall and back. Then you could have each team pool its loose change together to get exactly 41 cents. After the teams have completed a few "easy" tasks, explain all the other things they have to do to receive the prize.

Step 3

If you have fewer than six people in your group, try to get everyone involved in discussing these statements. After you read each statement, go around the group and have each person (not just volunteers) explain his or her reaction. Because of your small group, you have time to explore your group members' feelings. To get your kids to open up, you might ask questions like: **What Bible incidents or portrayals of Jesus in the media give you the idea that Jesus was kind of wimpy? If you knew that you were facing a horrible death in the future, do you think it would be hard to live your life day to day?**

Step 3

Rather than having group members work individually on the slips, work on them together as a group. For each slip, have one person read the assigned passage; have another person complete the first statement; and have another person complete the second statement. Then ask other group members if they have anything to add. Alternate assignments for each slip until you've completed all ten.

Step 1

Stage an elaborate production for the opening skit. Provide costumes for the two lead characters—a felt hat and leather jacket for Indy and an expensive-looking outfit for Cindy. Put a little makeup on the actors to make it look as though they've been through a rough adventure. Rather than having group members provide sound effects, try to find an appropriate sound-effects tape. Use rubber snakes, spiders, bats, rats, and bugs as props. (For extra effect, have the props attached to strings so that they can be maneuvered during skit.) If possible, the stage area should be dark enough to suggest a dangerous place, but light enough so that the audience can see what's going on. And, of course, no parody of Indiana Jones would be complete without the *Raiders of the Lost Ark* theme playing in the background.

Step 2

The larger your group, the better chance your group members will have of finding teammates. Set a time limit—perhaps two minutes—and award prizes to the teams that complete the assignment on time.

Step 2

To further explore your group members' opinions of Jesus, draw on some passages that they've probably heard many, many times in their lives. Have volunteers read aloud Matthew 5:5 and Matthew 5:39. Ask: **When you read of Jesus saying, "Blessed are the meek" and telling people to turn the other cheek to those who hurt them, how does that affect your opinion of Him? Why?**

Step 3

It might be helpful for your "jaded" group members to put themselves into each scene described in the passages on the slips. They've probably heard and read these passages dozens of times; so, as a change of pace, encourage them to *live* the passages. Have them imagine that they're with Jesus (perhaps as His disciples) in each situation. How would they be feeling? What would they advise Jesus to do?

Step 2

Task #2 assumes that most of your group members are Christians. If that's not the case, substitute the task with another situation that would require courage. For instance, you might use something like "Telling your father that you got an 'F' on your report card" or "Telling your mother that you broke her favorite lamp."

Step 3

If your group members don't have much Bible background, you may need to give them the full picture of Jesus and His work on earth. You need to explain that He was fully God and fully human at the same time. As God, He knew what His mission on earth was: to save mankind by taking upon Himself the punishment for the world's sins—a punishment that included physical torture and one of the most painful forms of execution imaginable. Because He was human, His body would experience the same kind of pain that we would experience under similar circumstances. Throughout His life, He knew the agony He would face; yet He had the courage to go through with it.

Step 2

Have group members pair up. Instruct them to talk with their partners about the scariest thing they've ever had to do. Have them explain why the situation was scary, how they felt at the time, and what happened. Then have them share how they managed to find the courage to face the situation. Be prepared to share a story of your own to get things started.

Step 5

Wrap up the session with a time of silent prayer. Have group members refer back to the slip(s) they were given from Repro Resource 8. Have them thank Jesus for making the choice He made and for not choosing to avoid danger or pain. Then group members should pray that Jesus would give *them* courage to face their scary or difficult situations.

Step 1
Instead of using Repro Resource 7 as a guy-girl skit, rename Indiana James as Young Wendy Fearless and have two girls play the roles. After the skit is concluded and the actors have been applauded, include these questions in the discussion. **Is courage easier for guys than for girls? Why or why not? Do you think courage has a different definition for girls? If so, what is it?**

Step 2
Before the session, write only the first two statements listed and leave #3 blank. As you begin "Courage Counters," ask your group members to think of some things that would be very difficult for them and would take a great amount of courage. Then, as a group, vote on one suggestion to use. Substitute that suggestion for #3, and continue with the activity.

Step 1
Rewrite the skit so that "Cindy" becomes "Lindy," Indy's younger brother. Lindy should act like a six year old throughout the skit. He should be scared of the various things in the temple, but rather than saying, "Eek!" and screaming, he should whine and say things like "I want my mommy." At the end of the skit, when Indy discovers his zit, Lindy should say, "What's wrong with having a zit? I thought all teenagers got zits!"

Step 2
This activity may not work well if your guys aren't willing to share honestly with each other about what scares them. For instance, their competitive, "macho" natures may prevent them from admitting that someone else could do one of the tasks for fewer "courage units" than they could. To avoid this problem, you might want to list the three tasks (and any other tasks you can think of that would require courage) on the board, and then have group members rank them according to how scary they would be for *most people*. Guys may be more willing to share if they don't have to admit their personal fears. By putting the emphasis on "most people's" fears, you'll probably get a better response from your group members.

Step 1
After the skit, play a game called "Guts." Bring in several different kinds of beverages—milk, cranberry juice, cola, coffee, egg nog, root beer, etc. Mix various combinations in a cup and then ask who has the "guts" to drink the concoction. For added effect, you might also want to bring in ketchup, mustard, mayonnaise, tobasco sauce, etc. to add to the mix. Use this activity to supplement your discussion of what it means to have courage (or "guts").

Step 4
Turn this into an active exercise instead of a theoretical one. Explain that you will be giving group members four assignments to complete. The assignments will require work, but the first person to complete all four of them will get a prize. The assignments are as follows: do twenty push-ups; run to the far wall and back ten times; do twenty sit-ups; do thirty jumping jacks. (Adjust the assignments as necessary to fit your group.) When the first person finishes all four assignments, make a big deal out of awarding him or her the worthless prize.

Step 1

Record several action sequences from TV shows. Make sure you get some spectacular scenes in which the stunt people probably put themselves at risk. Try to get scenes that include someone jumping or falling off a tall building, someone hanging from a helicopter, someone in a high-speed car chase, someone battling a dangerous animal, etc. After you play each scene, have group members rate on a scale of one to ten how much courage it would take to do a stunt like that.

Step 3

Rent a couple of movies that deal with the life of Jesus (*The Greatest Story Ever Told, Jesus*, etc.). Show a couple of scenes from the movies in which Jesus is portrayed as being gentle, meek, or "wimpy." Then have group members talk about how accurate they think the portrayals are.

Step 2

Distribute index cards to your group members. Read each task aloud. (Add some of your own, if possible. For instance, you might suggest "Reporting an older student who's selling drugs in your school," "Singing a solo in front of the whole church," etc.) After you read a task, group members will rate that task on a scale of one to ten according to how much courage the task would require (one equals very little courage; ten equals a lot of courage). Group members will write their scores on their index cards and display them like judges at gymnastics or ice-skating competitions do.

Step 3

Rather than having kids work on Repro Resource 8 individually or in small groups, go through the sheet together as a group. Read each Scripture passage aloud. Then ask one person to name a choice Jesus had in that passage to avoid danger or pain; ask another person to name the choice Jesus actually made.

Step 1

Make the Temple of Gloom a scary "crack house" or "hotel" Indy and Cindy are trying to get out of. Instead of Cindy being afraid of skeletons, fungus beetles, rattlesnakes, and the like, have her fear the asphyxiating and intoxicating smoke, sewer rats, roaches, slipping on crack vials, someone propositioning them to get high, and a drug dealer with a gun. These images may resonate clearer for some city youngsters.

Step 2

Some urban examples of courage for this activity might include:
1. Going into an inner-city housing development at night.
2. Preaching at an Hispanic or African-American Sunday service without preparation.
3. Telling a drug dealer to stop his evil deeds.
4. Stopping a riot.
5. Protesting a Ku Klux Klan rally in a racist neighborhood.
6. Using the high school bathroom.
7. Telling your father to stop beating your mother.

Step 2

Junior highers may be reluctant to honestly share in front of high schoolers how much courage it would take to do a certain task. If you think that might be the case with your group, skip playing the game. Simply collect the index cards and read (without revealing any identities) how group members divided the courage units.

Step 5

Some of your junior highers may be reluctant to share some of their scary situations for fear that the high schoolers will think their fears are childish. To prevent this, recruit a couple of your high schoolers before the activity to help you. Ask them to recall their junior high days and think about what was scary to them at that time in their lives. Then, during this closing activity, these high schoolers can mention the situations they recalled. Not only will this help your junior highers feel more comfortable about sharing their fears, it may also help bridge the gap between the two age groups.

Step 2

Change the list of challenges to be written before the session. Instead of using the campaign speech as #1, write, "Explaining at a school board meeting why your school should have more computers."

Step 3

Instead of using all of the slips from Repro Resource 8, choose five or six and eliminate the others. Have group members work in small groups to find the information asked for on the slip. As the groups report what they've written, take a little extra time describing the event and the choice Jesus had to make. Help your sixth graders identify with each situation as if they were present and observing the alternatives.

Date Used:

Approx.
Time

Step 1: Indy and Cindy _5-7min_
o Extra Action
o Large Group
o Mostly Girls
o Mostly Guys
o Extra Fun
o Media
o Urban
Things needed:

Step 2: Courage Counters _5-7min_
o Large Group
o Heard It All Before
o Little Bible Background
o Fellowship & Worship
o Mostly Girls
o Mostly Guys
o (Short Meeting Time)
o Urban
o Combined Junior High/High School
o Sixth Grade
Things needed: _index cards_

Step 3: Profile in Courage _10 min_
o Small Group (#1)
o Small Group (#2)
o Heard It All Before
o Little Bible Background
o Media
o Short Meeting Time
o (Sixth Grade)
Things needed: _photocopies;_
pencils

Step 4: Eyes on the Prize _____
o Extra Action
o Extra Fun
Things needed:

**Step 5: Breaking Down
the Door** _5-7min_
o Fellowship & Worship
o Combined Junior High/High School
Things needed: _Box; Candy;_
markers

Does He Really Love Me?

YOUR GOALS FOR THIS SESSION:

Choose one or more

- [ ] To help kids see that Jesus felt and demonstrated real, personal love when He was on earth.

- [ ] To help kids understand that Jesus loves them in ways they can measure, even if they don't always feel His love.

- [ ] To help kids identify and work on removing one barrier that keeps them from feeling Jesus' love.

- [ ] Other _____

Your Bible Base:

John 13–14
Romans 8:35-39
Ephesians 3:16-19

Love Scenes

(Needed: Paper bags; bubble gum; hair dryer; prizes)

Get two pairs of volunteers—a guy and a girl in each pair. Seat the two pairs at the front of the room.

Explain that you're going to conduct a Hollywood screen test. The guy and girl in each pair will act out a romantic scene. To make it easy, these will be the only lines of dialogue:

GUY: "Oh, Priscilla."

GIRL: "Oh, Pemberton."

The actors should use the lines over and over, trying to sound as romantic as possible.

Then add: **Oh, there's one other thing. To find out whether you can work around all the noise of a Hollywood set, I may add a couple of minor distractions. But keep going. The couple that sounds the most romantic will win the prize. Go!**

After pairs have said the lines a couple of times, start jumping in with distractions. Add each of the following every 15 seconds or so.

(1) Get a breeze going on the actors with a hand-held hair dryer.

(2) Add another actor, whose job is to bother the pairs by yelling things like, "Peanuts! Popcorn! Get your peanuts right here!"

(3) Give all the actors bubble gum and tell them that they must blow at least one bubble each.

(4) Put paper bags over the actors' heads.

After your actors have suffered enough, let the rest of the group choose the winning pair. Award prizes.

Then ask: **Do you think the actors did a good job of communicating true love to each other? Why or why not?** (Probably not—since they weren't really in love, they couldn't use their own words, and too many other things were going on.)

In real life, how can you tell whether somebody loves you? (He or she says so; the person does thoughtful things for you and treats you as if you're special; the person wants to spend time with you; etc.)

STEP 2

Jesus Loves Me?

Have kids sit in a circle if possible. Announce that you're going to sing (or say) the words to the song, "Jesus Loves Me." But each person can say only one word; the first says, "Jesus," the second says, "loves," etc., all the way around the circle until you've finished the first verse and chorus. Anyone who doesn't know the words should feel free not to participate.

When you're done singing or saying the song in this way, ask:

What was that all about? What's the message of that song? (That Jesus loves us.)

But what does that mean? *How* **does He love us?** Answers will vary; you don't need to settle on one answer yet.

According to this song, how do we know Jesus loves us? (The Bible tells us so.)

Is that the only way to know? Or can you feel His love?

Let kids respond if they want to. Then say: **We hear a lot about how Jesus loves us and how we're supposed to love Him— but many of us aren't sure exactly what that means. Let's find out.**

STEP 3

Let Me Count the Ways

(Needed: Bibles; cut-up copies of Repro Resource 9; team prize)

Before the meeting, copy and cut enough sets of cards from "Out of Order" (Repro Resource 9) so that you have one set of cards for every three or four kids. Put each set in a separate envelope, and shake each envelope to thoroughly mix up the order of the cards.

At this point, form teams of three or four kids. Give each team an envelope of cards. Announce that the first team to put its cards in the right order will be the winner. All the quotes are from John 13–14.

OPTIONS

Make sure each team has at least one New International Version of the Bible. Then say, **Go!**

Allow plenty of time for kids to scan the chapters and put their verses in order. Give a prize to the first team that puts its cards in the right order, or the team that gets the most done in seven minutes. (Note that the quotes appear in the correct order on the original Repro Resource 9.)

Then ask: **What do these quotes tell you about the kind of love Jesus has for people?**

As you work your way through the quotes, use the following information as needed.

"Having loved His own ..." (13:1)—Jesus loves specific people (here, His disciples), not just people in general. His love is also something He shows, not just something He feels.

"He poured water into a basin ..." (13:5)—His love makes Him willing to serve people, even doing the "low-down" jobs.

"One of them, the disciple whom Jesus loved ..." (13:23)—Again, Jesus loves specific people, has special feelings for them, and is willing to be close to them.

"As I have loved you ..." (13:34)—His love is an example of the way we should love each other.

"In my Father's house ..." (14:2)—Jesus' love makes Him interested in our futures, and He cares enough to prepare places in heaven for us.

"I will come back ..." (14:3)—Jesus loves us enough that He wants to have us with Him forever.

"You may ask me for anything ..." (14:14)—One way Jesus shows His love is by listening to our requests and answering them.

"I will ask the Father ..." (14:16, 17)—Jesus loves us enough to give us the guidance we need while He's away.

"I will not leave you as orphans ..." (14:18)—Because He loves us, He won't abandon us.

"Because I live ..." (14:19)—He loves us enough to give us eternal life. That's why He died on the cross for us.

"I am in my Father ..." (14:20)—He loves us enough to want to be part of us.

"He who loves me ..." (14:21)—He promises to love not just a few special friends, but anyone who loves and obeys Him.

"If anyone loves me ..." (14:23)—Jesus (and His Father) love us enough to live with and in us.

"Peace I leave with you ..." (14:27)—Jesus cares how we're feeling; He's interested in whether we are at peace or not.

"Do not let your hearts be troubled ..." (14:27)—He loves us enough to reassure and encourage us.

After discussing the quotes, ask: **Which of these quotes means the most to you? Why?**

STEP 4

Can You Feel It?

(Needed: Electric fan; crepe paper; tape)

Set up an electric fan at the front of the room. Kids should be far enough away from it that they won't feel the breeze. Turn on the fan.

Ask: **Is this fan off or on? How do you know?** (We saw you turn it on; we can hear it.)

Tape a few strips of crepe paper to the front of the fan, so that the breeze blows the strips. Ask: **Now how do you know whether the fan is on?** (We can see the paper moving.)

But you still can't feel it, can you? What would you have to do to feel whether the fan is on? (Get close to it.)

Choose one person to move closer to the fan until he or she can feel it. Then ask that person: **Is the fan off or on? How do you know?** (On; I can feel it.)

Now move closer to the fan until you can feel the breeze. Raise your hand as soon as you can feel it.

Wait until all the kids have raised their hands. **Now, when did the fan start blowing—when I turned it on, or when you raised your hand?** (When you turned it on.)

How might feeling the breeze from this fan be like feeling Jesus' love for us?

Listen to kids' responses. Then make the following points as needed.

(1) Just as the fan can be working even if we don't feel it, Jesus can be loving us even if we don't feel His love.

(2) We can tell from the Bible that Jesus loves us, just as we can tell from the blowing strips of paper that the fan is on—even if we don't feel it.

(3) We can listen to others who do feel Jesus' love, even when we can't.

(4) The closer we are to Jesus, the more we can feel His love—just as we felt the breeze as we got closer to the fan.

Have a volunteer read Ephesians 3:16-19. Then ask: **Do you think Paul, who wrote these verses, could feel Jesus' love?** (Yes; he seemed to know "how wide and long and high and deep" it is. Paul wanted his readers not only to know about Jesus' love, but to be full of His love in their hearts. Jesus' love is more than an intellectual thing—it surpasses knowledge.)

He was praying that all Christians would know that, too.

OPTIONS

LITTLE BIBLE BACKGROUND

MOSTLY GIRLS

URBAN

What things did he think would help them do that? (Having power from God's Holy Spirit; believing that Christ lives in our hearts; being "rooted" in love—so that we know what love is in the first place.)

STEP 5

Something's Come between Us

(Needed: Paper plates; markers or pens)

Pass out paper plates, one for each group member. Kids should still be standing close enough to the fan that they can feel the breeze.

Have kids hold the paper plates in front of their faces. Ask: **Can you still feel the breeze on your face? Why not?** (No; the plate is in the way.)

What are some things that keep us from feeling Jesus' love for us, just as the plates keep us from feeling the breeze? (Feeling guilty about something we've done, too guilty to get close to Jesus; not communicating with Him in prayer; keeping busy with lots of other things; being mad at Him because we think our prayers weren't answered; having doubts that we don't get answers to; etc.)

Hand out markers or pens. **On your plate, write or draw letters or symbols that stand for something that keeps you from feeling the love of Jesus. Then decide what you want to do with the plate. If you don't want to do anything about the problem that keeps you from feeling Jesus' love, you might keep the plate. If you want to get rid of the problem, you might sail the plate into a corner or tear it up.**

After giving kids a few moments to decide what to do, ask them to face the fan so that they can feel the breeze again. As they do, read Romans 8:35-39.

Then say: **Jesus' love for us is stronger than anything else. No one can take it from us. But He won't force His love on us if we don't want it.** Give kids a chance to pray silently, telling the Lord how they feel about His love and asking for His help in removing anything that keeps them from feeling that love.

Out of Order

"Having loved His own who were in the world, He now showed them the full extent of His love."

"He poured water into a basin and began to wash His disciples' feet, drying them with the towel that was wrapped around Him."

"One of them, the disciple whom Jesus loved, was reclining next to Him."

"As I have loved you, so you must love one another."

"In My Father's house are many rooms. . . .
I am going there to prepare a place for you."

"I will come back and take you to be with Me."

"You may ask Me for anything in My name, and I will do it."

"I will ask the Father, and He will give you another Counselor to be with you forever—the Spirit of truth."

"I will not leave you as orphans; I will come to you."

"Because I live, you also will live."

"I am in My Father, and you are in Me, and I am in you."

"He who loves Me will be loved by My Father, and I too will love him and show Myself to him."

"If anyone loves Me, he will obey My teaching. My Father will love him, and We will come to him and make Our home with him."

"Peace I leave with you; My peace I give you."

"Do not let your hearts be troubled and do not be afraid."

EXTRA ACTION

Step 3

For added excitement, turn this activity into a relay race. Give each team a roll of masking tape. Once team members have determined the order of the cards, they must take turns running the cards one at a time to the other end of the room and taping them to the wall. The first team to tape all fifteen cards to the wall in the correct order wins.

Step 5

After group members have drawn their symbols on their plates, place a trash can in the middle of the room. Have group members try to toss their plates into the can. Explain that getting the plate in the trash can represents getting rid of the obstacle. If group members don't hit the trash can on their first shot, they should stand where their plates land and try again. Point out that getting rid of the obstacles that prevent us from feeling Jesus' love isn't easy. It may take several tries, over long periods of time. We may think we've gotten rid of an obstacle, only to have it pop up again later. Therefore, we should constantly be prepared to remove such obstacles.

SMALL GROUP

Step 1

If you have fewer than seven or eight people in your group, this would be a great activity in which to involve *all* of them. Use only one pair of actors for the activity. Then have the rest of your group members take turns trying to distract the pair. You may want to brainstorm some additional distractions for group members to use (such as plugging the actors' noses while they talk) or let your group members come up with their own.

Step 3

Cut apart one copy of Repro Resource 9, and spread the cards on the floor in front of the group. Give group members six minutes to arrange the cards in order. If they complete the assignment in the allotted time, they get a prize; if not, they have to perform some kind of stunt (singing "The B-I-B-L-E" as loud as they can, making ugly faces in front of the entire group, etc.).

LARGE GROUP

Step 1

Stage an elaborate "production area" for your Hollywood screen test. Create a set—perhaps the living room of a house (with couches, tables, TV, etc.) or a street corner (with a lamppost, fire hydrant, etc.). Give your actors stage directions to follow as they recite their lines. You could also have props available for the actors to use. You might consider having romantic music playing in the background. Depending on how big your group is, use three or four pairs in your screen test. Encourage the people doing the distracting to use their creativity—and any props on hand—as they disrupt each scene. For instance, someone could turn up the volume of the background music so loud that the actors can't hear each other—or perhaps substitute a rap or heavy metal recording. If you use a living room set, someone else may come in, sit between the two actors, and pretend to watch TV.

Step 2

Have your kids form groups of six or seven. Each group should sit in a circle. The object of the activity is to create a "round" in singing "Jesus Loves Me." Have one group begin the song (with the first person in the group singing "Jesus," the second singing "loves," etc.). When the first group gets to the word "know," point to a second group to begin the song. When the second group gets to the word "know," point to a third group, and so on. Each group should keep repeating the song (maintaining the proper pace) until you give the signal to stop.

Step 3

Kids who've grown up in the church have heard expressions like "Jesus loves me" and "Jesus cares about me" so often that the words tend to lose their significance and meaning. Help these group members "redefine" these expressions by having them describe Jesus' feelings toward them—without using the words *love* or *care* (or any variation of the words). One way to do this would be to have group members create valentines that Jesus might send to us—without using the words *love* or *care* on the valentines.

Step 5

If no one mentions it, you may want to suggest that "overfamiliarity" may hinder us in experiencing Jesus' love. Kids who've been raised in the church and who've heard (over and over and over) powerful testimonies of what Jesus' love has done in the lives of others may tend to (a) experience His love vicariously through others rather than experiencing it firsthand, or (b) doubt the power of Jesus' love in their own lives because they haven't had any "dramatic" evidences of it.

Step 3

Some of your group members may have a hard time truthfully stating, "Jesus loves me, this I know." They may *not* know that Jesus loves them. And "for the Bible tells me so" may not be enough to convince them. You may need to review with your group members Jesus' ultimate proof of His love—His willingness to take the punishment that we deserved for our sin and to give His life for us. You could introduce the topic by reading John 15:13, 14 and asking: **Can you think of a better way to prove your love for someone than by dying to save that person?**

Step 4

For those group members unfamiliar with Scripture and Bible history, it might be interesting to hear the background of Paul, the writer of Ephesians—and the person testifying to the power of Jesus' love. Point out that Paul (then known as Saul) was feared by most early Christians because he was a leader in the movement to stamp out Christianity. (Christianity was illegal in the early part of the first century.) He was probably personally responsible for arresting, torturing, and killing many Christians. But after a powerful encounter with the risen Jesus, Paul's life turned completely around. He ended up writing most of the books in the New Testament and beginning several of the early churches. Emphasize that Jesus' life-changing love is still available today to *anyone*, regardless of his or her background.

Step 2

Have group members pair up. Instruct them to share with their partners about a time in their lives when they experienced Jesus' love. They may share about something dramatic, like a recovery from a serious injury; or they may share about something less dramatic, like a comfort they received from a certain Bible verse or song. Then have group members share with their partners about a time in their lives when they doubted Jesus' love for them. They may share about the death of a loved one, about feeling lonely all the time, etc. Encourage group members to be honest and candid with their partners.

Step 5

Close the session by singing "Jesus Loves Me" as a group again. However, in place of the phrase "for the Bible tells me so," have group members substitute a *specific* passage from the Bible (perhaps one of the verses from John 13–14) that reassures them of Jesus' love. For instance, someone might sing, "Jesus loves me, this I know, for *John 14:14* tells me so. . . ."

Step 1

Instead of a guy-girl skit, have three volunteers each try to convince the rest of the group that she is loved the most. Have the three girls use one of these statements, repeating it over and over with exaggerated, dramatic expression. "I know Jerry loves me because he sent me flowers." "I can tell Zack loves me; he says flowers aren't important enough for our love." "I know how much Chuck loves me when I read the poetry he writes about me." Use the same distractions, and then see how many group members are convinced by these statements about love.

Step 4

Have your group members talk about the frequent unreliability of human feelings. After using the fan as an illustration, have your group members divide into three teams. Give each team a set of the "Out of Order" slips. Give the teams two minutes to decide how many slips involve *doing* something to show love. Afterward, have someone read aloud II John 6 and John 15:9-14. Explain that Jesus' love for us is something that will never change.

Step 1

Instead of using two guy-girl pairs, use two pairs of guys. Explain that the pairs will be acting out a dramatic scene in a love story. Assign one person in each pair this line of dialogue: "I love her with all of my heart." Assign the other person in each pair this line: "You can't love her—I love her!" Use the same distractions, and then award a prize to the winning pair. Afterward, ask: **Do you think the actors did a good job of communicating their love for the girl? Why or why not? In real life, how can you tell whether somebody loves you?**

Step 5

Guys may be reluctant to write even letters or symbols on their plates for fear that someone else will see what they wrote and figure it out. So rather than having them write on their plates, have them *think* of something that prevents them from feeling Jesus' love. Then explain that the plate *represents* that obstacle.

Step 1

Open the session with a game of "If You Love Me." Have group members form a circle. Choose one person to be "it." That person will kneel in front of someone of the opposite sex and say, "If you love me, _____, smile." In addressing the victim, the person who is "it" should think of some goofy pet name to call the person—"Squirrel Cheeks," "Chicken Lips," "Honey Bunch," etc. The victim must then respond, "_____ (his or her pet name) loves you, but I just can't smile"—without smiling. If the victim smiles, he or she becomes "it"; if not, the person who is it must find another victim.

Step 2

After group members have recited the song normally, have a contest to see if they can recite it *backward*. Give them a minute to think of the lyrics. Then point to a person to begin. Going clockwise around the circle, group members will recite the words to the song in reverse order, one word at a time ("so," "me," "tells," "Bible," etc.). If a person says a wrong word or takes more than five seconds to think of the next word, he or she is out. Continue until only one person remains.

Step 1

Before the session, record several clips from TV shows, movies, commercials, or popular songs in which the word *love* is mentioned. Look for several different uses of the word. For instance, someone in a commercial might say, "I love what you do for me, Toyota" or "Quaker Oats—you're gonna love it in an instant." Characters in TV shows or movies might use the word love to describe their feelings about everything from a person to a pet to a particular flavor of ice cream. Most popular songs deal with the topic of love (although you'll want to be careful about which songs you choose to record). After your group members have seen and listened to the various clips, have them come up with a definition of love that can be applied to every usage you just saw or heard. Then discuss how that general, vague definition compares to Jesus' feelings for us.

Step 5

As your group members work, play a recording of "Silent Love" (from the album *Medals*) by Russ Taff. When kids finish their plates, encourage them to listen to the lyrics of the song. Have them think about *why* the Lord's love is "silent."

Step 1

Rather than using volunteers to disrupt the skit, do it yourself. Use the bubble gum distraction and the paper bag distraction. Also, you might want to startle the actors a couple of times by yelling or jumping at them while they speak. Don't let the skit go on too long—60-90 seconds would be ideal.

Step 3

If you're running short of time, don't distribute Repro Resource 9. Instead, call out the Scripture references one at a time. Group members will then race to look up each passage and read aloud the quote that talks about Jesus' love.

Step 2

Expand the issue of love for your final question. Ask: **How do you know if Jesus loves the city?** Point out that people tend to look down on the city as a bad place to live. This false image has to be broken first among its inhabitants. Cause the group to wrestle with what godly things their city has to offer the kingdom of God. Some may recognize churches, the youth group, a quiet park or stream. Others may acknowledge the multiplicity of the city or elders in their communities as a blessing. Still another may notice the animals (squirrels and pigeons) that inhabit the city. Let group members know that Jesus loves the city, and can be found just as powerfully there if we search Him out.

Step 4

Have a volunteer go to the other side of the room and put either cologne or perfume on—just enough so that it's obvious he or she has it on. Instruct this person to stand away from the fan. Ask the rest of the group members to determine whether he or she is wearing cologne or perfume. The group members should not be able to answer. Then have the person stand in front of the fan. Eventually, the group will be able to describe the aroma and identify if it's cologne or perfume. Have group members slowly move closer and notice how the fragrance pleasantly intensifies. Then discuss how the Holy Spirit (wind) moves from the Son (the volunteer) through the power of God (the fan) to alert the world of the "aroma" of Christ.

Step 1

If possible, use two high schoolers for one pair of actors and two junior highers for the other pair. Then have a junior higher try to distract the high school pair and have a high schooler try to distract the junior high pair. The high schooler doing the distracting might say things like, "You two are too young to be in love! You're just little kids!" The junior higher doing the distracting might say things like, "If you're in love with him, why are you wearing _____'s letter jacket?" If you don't think the rest of the group can be objective in determining a winner, you may need to choose the winning pair yourself.

Step 3

This activity would work well as a competition between junior highers and high schoolers. Split up the two age groups and give one set of cards to each team. The first team to arrange all fifteen cards in order wins. To "raise the stakes" in the competition, you may want to announce that the losing team has to sing "You Win and We Lose" (to the tune of "Happy Birthday to You") to the winning team.

Step 1

Instead of using guy-girl pairs for a love scene, ask three or four volunteers to sit in front of the room and mime the facial expressions and actions they would use to show their love to someone (exaggerating as necessary). Use the distractions described in the session to interrupt your volunteer mimes. Afterward, take a vote to see who best expressed love.

Step 3

Help your sixth graders be more specific in their discussion of how Jesus expressed His love. As you talk about the quotes from John 13–14, summarize on the board the key ideas from each quote. For example, you might write, "Jesus shows His love by loving individuals, doing everyday jobs, caring about our future, listening, etc."

Date Used: _____

Approx. Time

Step 1: Love Scenes _____
o Small Group
o Large Group
o Mostly Girls
o Mostly Guys
o Extra Fun
o Media
o Short Meeting Time
o Combined Junior High/High School
o Sixth Grade
Things needed:

Step 2: Jesus Loves Me? _5min_
o Large Group
o Fellowship & Worship
o Extra Fun
o Urban
Things needed:

Step 3: Let Me Count the Ways _10-12min_
o Extra Action
o Small Group
o Heard It All Before
o Little Bible Background
o Short Meeting Time
o Combined Junior High/High School
o Sixth Grade
Things needed: _Photocopies_

Step 4: Can You Feel It? _5-7min_
o Little Bible Background
o Mostly Girls
o Urban
Things needed: _electric fan_
crepe paper tape

Step 5: Something's Come between Us _5min_
o Extra Action
o Heard It All Before
o Fellowship & Worship
o Mostly Guys
o Media
Things needed: _paper plates_
markers

Custom Curriculum Critique

Please take a moment to fill out this evaluation form, rip it out, fold it, tape it, and send it back to us. This will help us continue to customize products for you. Thanks!

1. Overall, please give this *Custom Curriculum* course (*Face to Face with Jesus*) a grade in terms of how well it worked for you. (A=excellent; B=above average; C=average; D=below average; F=failure) Circle one.

   A   B   C   D   F

2. Now assign a grade to each part of this curriculum that you used.

a. Upfront article	A	B	C	D	F	Didn't use
b. Publicity/Clip art	A	B	C	D	F	Didn't use
c. Repro Resource Sheets	A	B	C	D	F	Didn't use
d. Session 1	A	B	C	D	F	Didn't use
e. Session 2	A	B	C	D	F	Didn't use
f. Session 3	A	B	C	D	F	Didn't use
g. Session 4	A	B	C	D	F	Didn't use
h. Session 5	A	B	C	D	F	Didn't use

3. How helpful were the options?
   - ❏ Very helpful
   - ❏ Somewhat helpful
   - ❏ Not too helpful
   - ❏ Not at all helpful

4. Rate the amount of options:
   - ❏ Too many
   - ❏ About the right amount
   - ❏ Too few

5. Tell us how often you used each type of option (4=Always; 3=Sometimes; 2=Seldom; 1=Never)

	4	3	2	1
Extra Action	❏	❏	❏	❏
Combined Jr. High/High School	❏	❏	❏	❏
Urban	❏	❏	❏	❏
Small Group	❏	❏	❏	❏
Large Group	❏	❏	❏	❏
Extra Fun	❏	❏	❏	❏
Heard It All Before	❏	❏	❏	❏
Little Bible Background	❏	❏	❏	❏
Short Meeting Time	❏	❏	❏	❏
Fellowship and Worship	❏	❏	❏	❏
Mostly Guys	❏	❏	❏	❏
Mostly Girls	❏	❏	❏	❏
Media	❏	❏	❏	❏
Extra Challenge (High School only)	❏	❏	❏	❏
Sixth Grade (Jr. High only)	❏	❏	❏	❏

6. What did you like best about this course?

7. What suggestions do you have for improving *Custom Curriculum*?

8. Other topics you'd like to see covered in this series:

9. Are you?
   ❑ Full time paid youthworker
   ❑ Part time paid youthworker
   ❑ Volunteer youthworker

10. When did you use *Custom Curriculum*?
    ❑ Sunday School   ❑ Small Group
    ❑ Youth Group   ❑ Retreat
    ❑ Other _____

11. What grades did you use it with? _____

12. How many kids used the curriculum in an average week? _____

13. What's the approximate attendance of your entire Sunday school program (Nursery through Adult)? _____

14. If you would like information on other *Custom Curriculum* courses, or other youth products from David C. Cook, please fill out the following:

Name: _____
Church Name: _____
Address: _____
_____

Phone: (_____) _____

Thank you!